# MEDIA STUDIES

## An Introduction

## Brian Dutton

### with John Mundy

LONGMAN

**For Susan**

Longman Group UK Limited,
*Longman House, Burnt Mill, Harlow,
Essex CM20 2JE, England
and Associated Companies throughout the
world.*

Published in the United States of America
by Longman Inc., New York.

First published 1989
Fifth impression 1993

*Designed by Ken Brooks
Set in 10/13$^1$/$_2$ point Century Schoolbook
Produced by Longman Singapore Publishers Pte Ltd
Printed in Singapore*

ISBN 0 582 02449 8

**British Library Cataloging in
Publication Data**

Dutton, Brian, 1952–
  Media Studies: an introduction
  1. Great Britain. Educational
  institutions.
  Curriculum subjects: Mass media
  I. Title   II. Mundy, John
  302.234071041
  ISBN 0-582-02449-8

The Publisher's policy is to use paper manufactured
from sustainable forests.

# CONTENTS

**Source 1.1**

## What are the media?

***Source 1.1***
From source 1.1, try to list as many examples of the media as possible (e.g. *The Fourth Protocol* is a film).

What they all share is an ability to reach large public audiences via print, film, sound, etc.

***Source 1.1***

# Why study the media?

Consider how much a part the media plays in our daily lives. Here are three 'diaries' written by 15–17 year old students describing how the media fits into a typical weekday.

## Activities

1. Write a similar diary for a typical weekday, describing the time you spend with the different media.
2. Try to calculate how many hours you spend in an average week:
   a. Watching television/ video
   b. Listening to the radio
   c. Reading magazines and newspapers
   d. Listening to records and tapes.

Many adults are unhappy about the time young people spend with the media. Most children spend more hours in front of their television set than they do in the classroom. In fact, the average adult in Britain spends between 25–75 hours each week with the media (depending on how strict a definition is used, e.g. if the radio is on, is it being listened to?).

Consider the example of television in the home. This is likely to occupy more time than any other media.

---

**Lisa – age 15**

| | |
|---|---|
| 7.30 a.m. | Fall out of bed, get dressed. |
| 7.40 a.m. | Go downstairs, eat my breakfast and listen to Radio 2 – not my choice. |
| 7.55 a.m. | Go into bathroom. |
| 8.05 a.m. | Dry my hair while listening to music centre, usually Jerico tape. |
| 8.20 a.m. | Put contact lenses in, switch to Radio 1 and listen to Mike Smith's breakfast show. |
| 8.30 a.m. | Have a quick flick through the *Sun*, read 'Striker' and my horoscope, then go and catch my bus. |
| 4.20 p.m. | Arrive home from school, read the *Sun* to see what's on TV tonight. Then read *Just Seventeen* and have a cup of tea. |
| 5.00 p.m. | Watch *John Craven's Newsround* and children's serial whilst having tea. |
| 6.00 p.m. | Start homework and listen to tapes or radio, or sometimes go to a friends to watch a video like *Friday Night Live*. |
| 9.00 p.m. | Have shower, wash hair. |
| 10.30 p.m. | Watch TV in bed or read a book. |

**Karen – age 16**

| | |
|---|---|
| 7.25 a.m. | I wake up to the sounds of Mike Smith on Radio 1. I wash in the bathroom and then go downstairs to wash my hair. |
| 7.40 a.m. | I eat my breakfast in front of *Breakfast Time* and depending on whether I have already read it, I read yesterday's newspaper. |
| 7.50 a.m. | I go back upstairs to get ready for college and listen to Mike Smith trying to be a DJ and a game host for 'Fantazia' till 8.30. |
| 4.10 p.m. | I arrive home, the television is already on signifying that my younger sister is home. I may then start some homework or watch Children's BBC depending on the urgency of the work. |
| 5.35 p.m. | I watch *Neighbours*, and then listen to the 6 o'clock news and weather forecast whilst having dinner. After dinner I do some homework whilst listening to my walkman. |
| 7.30 p.m. | I usually watch *EastEnders*, or else stay in my room listening to music. |
| 9.00 p.m. | I go downstairs and watch whatever my parents have on TV. |
| 11.00 p.m. | I go to bed. |

**Darren – age 17**

| | |
|---|---|
| 7.15 a.m. | Get up and switch on the radio (Capital Radio). |
| 8.15 a.m. | Switch off radio, listen to tape on walkman during journey to college (¾ hour), this cuts out the boring thought of a day at college. |
| 1 hour depending on what time my free period is, I listen to my walkman again. | |
| 12.40 p.m. | About 20 minutes during dinner break, I listen to my walkman. |
| 3.50 p.m. | Listen to walkman during journey home (¾ hour). You have to relax after a (hard) day at college! |
| 4.40 p.m. | Watch television (1½ hours). Can't miss *Neighbours*. |
| 6.10 p.m. | Read *Daily Mirror* which my dad brings in from work (½ hour). A nice bit of scandal before homework. |
| 6.40 p.m. | Listen to music from midi system (20 minutes). |
| 7.00 p.m. | Watch TV while eating dinner and after (3 hours). |
| 10.00 p.m. | Listen to radio while in bed (1 hour) – Essex Radio. |

1. Why do you think the bedroom is the second most popular place to have a TV set?
2. What might be the effects of homes having more than one TV set?
3. Select any one of the TV related equipment listed in source 1.2 and write a short account of how it may be used in the home.

If television and other media, like newspapers and radio, take so much of our time, then it is important to ask why this is so.

Do the media shape the way we think?
What do we learn about the world through the media?
Why are they so pleasurable for millions of people?
Who owns and controls the media?

These are some of the questions which make it so important to study the media.

## Viewing and Listening in the Home

Television is virtually a universal feature of people's lives. In all, 99% of our 1987 sample said they had a set at home. Notably these findings show a continuation of the trend towards multiple set ownership seen in previous years; nearly six out of ten of the adult population claim to have more than one television set at home. Indeed, triple set households are not uncommon – 17% of the 1987 sample said they had three television sets.

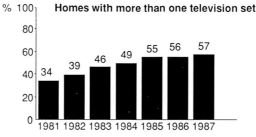

The location of TV sets within the home also shows change, as would be expected from this growth in the numbers of sets. Virtually everyone has a set in the main living room, while the next most popular location is a bedroom (24%). Fewer than one in ten has a set in the kitchen, or a dining room, or in any other room. As in previous years it seems that, by and large, television sets are used as fixed rather than as movable appliances – less than one in ten viewers said that any of their sets was not kept in one place. The growth in second (or third) sets is primarily due to sets in bedrooms.

As a device used simply to receive off-air broadcasts, a television set is used for about five hours a day on average, allowing in principle for further use of a relatively expensive piece of domestic equipment. Nowadays there exists a range of accessories and enhancements which can be used in conjunction with a 'basic' television set – video recorders, video disc players, teletext and viewdata services, video games and home computers. There are also alternative sources of programming such as cable and satellite.

**TV-related equipment in the home**

| | All adults | | | Adults with children | | |
|---|---|---|---|---|---|---|
| | 1985 % | 1986 % | 1987 % | 1985 % | 1986 % | 1987 % |
| Home | | | | | | |
| Video recorder | 38 | 44 | 55 | 51 | 58 | 69 |
| Home computer | 18 | 21 | 23 | 33 | 36 | 40 |
| Teletext | 17 | 17 | 23 | 17 | 20 | 24 |
| Video games | 9 | 10 | 10 | 15 | 17 | 16 |
| Cable TV | 1 | 1 | 1 | 2 | 1 | 2 |
| Video camera | 1 | 2 | 1 | 1 | 3 | 1 |
| Video disc players | * | 1 | 1 | * | 1 | 2 |
| Prestel/Viewdata | * | 1 | 1 | * | 1 | 1 |
| Satellite receiver | NA | NA | * | NA | NA | * |
| Have one or more of these | 50 | 57 | 65 | 68 | 74 | 82 |
| Have none of these | 50 | 43 | 35 | 32 | 26 | 18 |

(*less than 0.5%)   (NA = not asked)

(IBA, *Airwaves,* Winter 1987/8)

**Source 1.2**  Television in the home

## Making sense of the media. Case study: Madonna

Between 1985 and 1987, the pop singer Madonna achieved great success in the media. For example, she was the top selling record artist in 1986 with six top 20 hits, and three top 40 albums. She starred in films such as *Desperately Seeking Susan* and *Shanghai Surprise*, and appeared on countless magazine covers. The popular press regularly featured stories about her personal life.

How can we make sense of this success within media studies?

### 1. The image

*Source 1.3*
This picture has been described as the 'Madonna look'. What does this 'look' mean to you? Comment on Madonna's pose, her clothes, jewellery, hairstyles, etc.

Source 1.3

*Source 1.4*
Compare these two pictures of Madonna and film star Marilyn Monroe, who made a great impact in the 1950s and early 1960s (until 1962 when she died of a drug overdose) with her combination of sexuality and innocence.
1. What do they have in common?
2. How do they differ?

Source 1.4

## 2. Views about Madonna

### Source 1.5
Contrast the views of those who criticise Madonna with those who admire her. Why do you think such different views exist?

Clearly different interpretations of Madonna's image and popularity are possible. Much depends on who the audience is, and how they have made sense of Madonna through the music, videos, films, magazines, etc. Each of these media add to the overall image and meaning, but finally it is the audience which makes sense of Madonna.

Rock star Madonna was under a blistering attack from two top psychiatrists yesterday.

One branded her a 'pied piper of depravity'. And the other said her act projected the image of a tramp and a street-walker.

Dr Sam Jamus, a professor at New York Medical College, accused the singer – who wears crucifixes and black underwear on stage – of misleading a whole generation of girl fans.

'Madonna is a corrupting pied piper leading impressionable young girls down the primrose path to a depraved and degrading lifestyle,' he said.

'The sexually-explicit lyrics of her brash and vulgar songs advocate prostitution. She is blatantly selling the idea to America's young women that casual sex is not only OK, but even better is to get paid for it.'

Another professor, Dr Denilo Ponce, of Hawaii, said of Madonna, 24: 'The whole image she projects is that of a tramp – a street-walker eager to sell her favours to the highest bidder.'

A spokesman for Madonna said: 'That is the opinion of these two alleged experts. But the fans seem to like her.'

*Source 1.5a* (*Daily Star*, 12 Aug. 1985)

'She's sexy but she doesn't need men . . . She's kind of there all by herself.' 'She gives us ideas. It's really women's lib, not being afraid of what guys think.'

*Source 1.5b* (*Time*, May 1985)

Louisa Canon, 14, says she's one of Madonna's most committed fans. "I think she's wonderful. I love dressing like her. It just makes me feel good and full of confidence. Madonna's such a strong personality – she's done exactly what she wants and that's the way I'd like to be. The best things about her are her clothes and her husband. He's gorgeous."

Andrew Morley, 17, reckons he'd much rather sell T-shirts at the Madonna concert than have to sit through the show. "I think she's terrible. She's got such a slutty image and she tries hard to emulate Marilyn Monroe and fails miserably. She's just a big fuss about nothing."

*Source 1.5c* (*Just Seventeen*, Sept. 1987)

## 3. Madonna as a media product

The audience can only make sense of what is made available in the media. In the case of Madonna, someone had to decide to record her, write about her, film her, etc.

### Source 1.6

1. In what forms is Madonna being 'sold' as a product in the illustration below?
2. To what extent do you think that performers like Madonna can be sold to the public like breakfast cereals or motor cars?

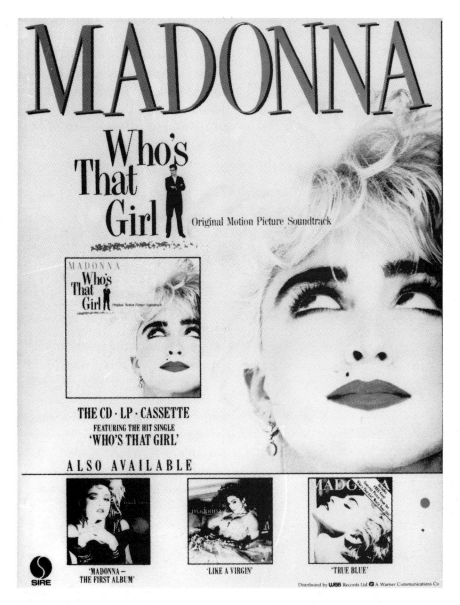

*Source 1.6*

### Key areas of study

**1.** *Language*
How do images, sounds and words create meaning in the media?

**2.** *Institution*
What factors shape the production and circulation of media output like television programmes, newspapers, films etc?

**3.** *Representation*
How do the media make sense of the world?
What ideas, beliefs and attitudes are portrayed?

**4.** *Genre*
What are the distinctive styles and forms of media content?

**5.** *Audiences*
Who are they and how do they make sense of the media?

These questions are not totally separate. In fact, many points crop up in more than one chapter. Like a jigsaw, each part of the picture only makes sense when fitted to another part.

### Practical work

Throughout the book, the emphasis is on an active approach to media studies. Stimulus sources are provided for discussion, and practical activities suggested, which may be done individually or in groups.
   Chapter 7 involves a full assessment of how to go about practical media work, especially in relation to coursework assignments.

# 2 LANGUAGE

*Source 2.1 a*    *(The World of Escher,* Collins)

*Source 2.2*

## Perception

'Things are not what they seem.'

*Source 2.1*   Perspectives
What can you see in these images?

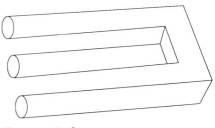

*Source 2.1b*

They seem to be playing tricks on our vision. That is because our minds insist we see the objects in a particular way. We have learned to see pictures according to certain rules of perspective. Both these images have broken those rules, and thus make it difficult for us to make sense of them.

*Source 2.2*
Can you see both the young and the old woman in this picture?

It is difficult to see both images without some effort – in this case, the young woman's chin is the old woman's nose. What we are doing is **reading the image** – providing our own interpretation of what it means.

# Semiology

This is the study of the meaning of signs (sometimes called semiotics).

## Source 2.3
What do each of these signs mean?

Although they may seem obvious to you, each sign has come to mean very different things to different people. The skull and crossbones has its roots in piracy, since when it has come to represent a warning against poison and, more recently, has been used in a TV cartoon for children. The swastika in ancient times was used religiously to symbolise the power of God or nature. The German Nazi party adopted it in the 1930s, so that it became linked to fascist politics. Closer to today, youth groups such as hells angels and punks have used it to decorate their clothes, whilst others have revived it as a signifier of their racial hatred of ethnic minorities in Britain. Such signs do not in themselves mean anything. People give them meaning, and it is the study of such meanings which is the purpose of semiology. A **sign** can be any physical form to which we give meaning, including words, pictures, colours, clothes, etc. For example, the word 'bad' commonly means evil or wicked. However, in black American street culture, it has come to mean good (as used in the title of Michael Jackson's 1987 LP). The colour red might mean communism or danger.

### Activity

1. Choose a colour and suggest what meaning(s) it has in our culture.
2. Choose a word which has more than one meaning (indicating it has changed).

**Source 2.3**  Skull and crossbones, swastika

**Source 2.4**

A sign such as a word or image is composed of two parts:

a. The physical form – that which we can see or hear. This is called the **signifier.**
b. The meaning of the form, which is the **signified**. For example, when we see a blue flashing light on top of a white car (two signifiers) we think it is a police car (what is signified).

What are the signifiers which appear on cards to make us think it is Christmas time?

Signs work together to create meaning.

### Source 2.4  *TV Times*

1. What are the signifiers on this *TV Times* cover?
2. What do they mean when added together?

Signs cannot be combined purely at random if they are to mean anything. They are combined according to certain rules, which form a **code**. For instance, traffic lights change colour in a standard sequence. Imagine the chaos if the red, amber and green lights switched at random! We learn to read signs according to codes (in the case of traffic lights, the highway code). Reading a book is no different. Words are combined according to the rules of spelling and grammar. When we read a sentence, we are **decoding** the meaning. All signs have to be decoded to be understood. Whilst reading a book, you are decoding the meaning of the words in the text. In the media, not only books count as texts, but anything made of signs like photographs, TV programmes, adverts, records and magazines. A **text** is any collection of signs whose meaning can be decoded.

***Source 2.5***  Peugeot advert
This is an advert for a car. What aspect of the car is being signified?

***Source 2.5***

*a* 'Police thugs at work'

*b* 'You're never alone with a Strand' (cigarette)

*Source 2.6*

*c*

## Images and words

Images and words are both examples of signs. An image by itself may have many 'different' meanings. An X can mean any of the following: wrong, crossroads and a kiss. The more uncertain the meaning of a sign, the more **open** it is. If an image is supplied with a written message, its meaning becomes more precise or **closed**. The words provide a reading or interpretation – they **anchor** the meaning of an image.

*Source 2.6*
How do the words 'anchor' the meaning of the pictures?

Most images are open to a variety of interpretations. In semiology, when an image can mean different things to people, it is said to be **polysemic**. There may well be an intended or **preferred meaning** supplied by whoever has provided the media text, but this may not be the same as how the audience reads the text. For example, for several years, BBC portrayed Alf Garnett as a racist bigot in the comedy series *Till Death Us Do Part* and later in *In Sickness and Health* with the intention of making audiences laugh *at* him. However, it is clear many viewers laughed *with* him, enjoying his prejudices, and thus reinforcing their own at the same time.

It may even be possible to change the meanings of media texts by adding your own message.

**Source 2.7**
1. How have the added messages changed the meanings of these adverts?
2. Why do you think this has been done?

*Source 2.7*

## Media codes

Television, radio, newspapers and other forms of the media use certain codes for creating meaning. These codes are based on rules and conventions, which have become recognised by audiences over time. A convention means a way of doing something which is generally accepted. In everyday life, we are surrounded by conventions such as shaking hands when meeting someone, or eating a meal with a knife and fork.

What are the codes and conventions associated with the different media?

### 1. Photography

A photograph appears to be a true record of life. The camera does not lie, but taking a picture does mean making choices, which can change the meaning of the picture. These include choosing the moment to take a shot, and deciding what to include or leave out (this is called framing the picture). There are also choices regarding aspects like lighting, focusing, angle of view and whether to use black and white or colour film. The camera sees the world differently from human vision, as can be seen in the photographs on the next page.

*Source 2.8* Photographic codes Describe what you can see in each of the pictures. What is being drawn to our attention? Comment on the lighting, focusing, angle and framing in each picture.

*Source 2.8*

## 2. Newspaper language

When reading newspapers it is possible to identify a variety of codes. All newspapers follow the rule that the most important story is presented on the front page near the top, usually accompanied by a picture. Even this rule has not always applied. The front page of *The Times* used to only carry classified adverts.

**Source 2.9**   The *Sun* and the *Independent*
How does the language of these two newspapers differ? Comment on: the headlines, layout, choice of words, length of sentence and story, the details provided and the use of quotes.

*Source 2.9a*

# THE INDEPENDENT

NEWSPAPER OF THE YEAR AWARD

No 373    FRIDAY 18 DECEMBER 1987    Published in London    25p

Backbenchers warn of dire consequences at next election if Government presses ahead

## Poll tax rebels defy plea for loyalty

**By Colin Hughes**
Political Correspondent

AT LEAST 30 backbench Tory MPs were last night preparing to rebel against the poll tax, seriously denting the "flagship" of the Conservative general election manifesto at its Commons launch.

Some rebels were predicting that the Government faced the sharpest second reading reduction in its 103-seat overall majority since the Shops Bill was defeated in the last Parliament — and that did not form a central plank of government policy.

They hoped that the rebellion would swell to at least 40 backbench Tories willing to display dissent. That would signal to the House of Lords that the Government's majority on its pro- ...

HERBIE KNOTT

### COMMONS SKETCH
## Rating value of MPs' addresses

**By Mark Lawson**

THE POLL TAX has led to an obsession with MPs' addresses. Paul "Two Mansions" Channon will, it has been noted, do rather well, as will prudent lady pensioners with retirement villas in Dulwich. But, as yesterday's second reading made clear, the new tax also stands to produce winners and losers of a different kind. The rateable value of members is fluctuating wildly.

## Mistakes blamed for baby's death

**By Anne Spackman**

PROFESSIONAL mistakes and administrative incompetence were the key factors which led to the death of Tyra Henry, the report into the baby's death, published today, concludes.

Tyra was murdered by her father Andrew Neil while in the care of Lambeth Council in south London. Her body was covered with bruises and 57 human bite marks, her skull was cracked and her brain damaged. Neil, 23, is serving a life sentence in Grendon Underwood psychiatric prison.

## Husak quits amid hopes of Czech reform

**From Patricia Koza**
of United Press International

PRAGUE — Gustav Husak, under whose leadership Czechoslovakia resisted the political and economic reforms of Mr Gorbachev, resigned yesterday as general secretary of the Communist Party.

Mr Husak, 74, who had ruled Czechoslovakia since Soviet tanks helped crush a fledgling reform movement in the Prague Spring of 1968, was immediately replaced by the Central Committee secretary, Milos Jakes, 55, chairman of the Central Committee's National Economic Commission, supervising economic restructuring plans.

**Moscow's servant quits, page 8**

---

### SUMMARY

**Jobless total falls again**

UNEMPLOYMENT fell sharply last month, with the seasonally-adjusted total dropping by 63,500 to 2,648,800. It was the seventeenth consecutive monthly decline. ... **Page 20**

**BBC fails**
The High Court refused to lift a temporary injunction preventing broadcast of the BBC Radio programme *My Country, Right or Wrong* ... **Page 3**

**Kasparov losing**
Garry Kasparov is on the verge of losing his world chess title as, with one game to go, he trails Anatoly Karpov by 11 games to 12 ... **Page 3**

**Art mystery**
Two of the most expensive pictures sold at auction have appeared in the Zurich Kunsthaus. But who owns them? Geraldine Norman examines the mystery ... **Page 5**

**Korean dilemma**
The most delicate and dangerous problem facing Korea's president-elect, Roh Tae Woo, is his relationship to the incumbent ... **Page 10**

**Bhopal payout**
Union Carbide has been ordered by an Indian court to pay £150m as interim compensation to the victims of the Bhopal gas ... **Page 10**

**Trial vendetta**
The body of the second man to be murdered since the end of Sicily's largest anti-Mafia trial was found by police ... **Page 10**

**Paper threatened**
South Africa's foremost anti-apartheid newspaper, *The Weekly Mail*, is threatened with government closure ... **Page 10**

### INSIDE

LIVING:
The roots of Jamaica ......... 14

FASHION:
Dressing the naked nape ............... 15

GARLAND:
Art of the political cartoon .......... 17

AUSTRALIA:
Ghosts at the bicentennial feast ............... 17

### CONTENTS

---

16    LANGUAGE

Source 2.9b

# THE Sun

Friday, December 18, 1987     20p     TODAY'S TV IS ON PAGE 16

## I LOVE YOUR AFTER-SHAVE CHARLES, SAYS KISS GIRL SUE

*Charles—lady-killing lotion*

SEE PAGE 7

# TV CHARMER DUMPS MISSUS

*Alexander . . . heart stopped*

## Hospital battery blunder killed our baby

**By JOHN KAY**

A NEW-BORN baby died because vital hospital equipment had a flat battery, a grieving couple claimed last night.

Parents Tony and Vicki Davies said their tot, Alexander, might have lived but for crucial minutes lost because of cut-backs in the maternity unit.

Vicki, 38, said she was connected to a monitoring machine at the Royal Berkshire Hospital, Reading, when she was about to give birth.

### Heart

She said: "Nothing showed up. I heard the doctor say they thought the battery was flat.

"That's when the panic started. They plugged me into another monitor. It showed the baby's heart had stopped and forceps were used to deliver him."

Alexander was revived but died two days later.

Tony, 38, of Newtown Common, Berks, said: "Our baby's death was directly due to lack of care and shortage of staff and facilities."

Health chiefs have ordered an inquiry.

**TRINGO BINGO! Today's numbers -Page 32**

*The mistress . . . Polly Bloomfield in her days as a model*

*The wife . . . TV star Nigel "The Charmer" Havers with Carolyn, the woman he left behind*

**By SUE CARROLL and STUART HIGGINS**

TV star Nigel "The Charmer" Havers has left his wife for his stunning blonde mistress, The Sun can reveal today.

Handsome Havers, 36, moved out of his family home to share the swish London flat of former Sixties model Polly Bloomfield—his secret love for four years.

He left behind his wife of 12 years, 41-year-old Carolyn, and their nine-year-old daughter Katie.

Only last month, Havers—

## Lovenest with blonde

### EXCLUSIVE

who played a love 'em and leave 'em conman in ITV's hit series The Charmer—fiercely **DENIED** rumours of an affair.

But a close friend of wealthy socialite Polly, 36—the estranged wife of property heir John Bloomfield—said last night:

- Polly and Nigel are desperately in love. They have tried to end the affair—Polly had even met another man. But their love wouldn't die.

They had been seeing one another for about four years, but it was always on and off.

This time it looks as if it's for real.

Polly is a very beautiful woman who could have any man she wanted, but she can't get Nigel out of her head.

Havers—son of former Attorney General Sir Michael—lived

Continued on Page Two

### 3. Radio language

Radio is an **auditory** medium – it depends entirely on sound. Much is left to the imagination of the listener. There are a range of auditory signifiers for creating meaning. These include:

**a.** *Words*
This is the obvious language of radio. Different types of speaker may be signified by the tone of voice or speed of delivery. For example, a rural accent may be used to represent simplicity or lack of sophistication. A French or Italian voice may signify romance and charm.

**b.** *Sounds*
Sound effects are often used to create atmosphere and signify context where things are happening. Crying seagulls suggest the seaside, twittering birds the countryside, and roaring traffic the city streets. The sound of approaching footsteps, followed by a creaking door, may create suspense. Sounds may be faded in and out to signify passing time.

**c.** *Music*
This may also create mood, as it does in film and television. Usually it is played for its own enjoyment or as a jingle for linking or introducing programmes.

---

#### Activities

1. Listen to 20 minutes of radio drama, make a note of all the sound effects used to signify the setting and events taking place.
2. Listen to the speakers' voices on each of the BBC channels and local radio in an evening. Are there any differences in their speech such as accent, tone, speed of delivery?
   For a further discussion of practical work with radio see pages 133–6.

---

### 4. Film and television language

How can film or television be thought of as a language? Unlike written and spoken language, there are no strict rules for creating meaning in film and video. Pop music videos have shown that virtually any combination of images can be shown with the music.

However, there are certain codes of language in film making which audiences have learned to read. Watching television may seem like looking through a 'window on the world' in which the screen simply reveals what is there, but the images have been carefully selected in order to create certain meanings. What is seen is just as much a construction or product as a book or magazine written by an author. As with photography, there are many choices of shot for filming a subject. What we see on film is normally much narrower a field of vision than our own, which is roughly 180°. Try stretching out your arms and look straight ahead. You should just be able to see your arms out of the corner of your eyes.

The camera is therefore selective. What kinds of choices are possible?

**a.** *Shot distance*
This affects what we can see and how closely involved we become with a subject.

*Source 2.10*
1. Select three of these shots, and explain why they are selected for use in film or television.
2. Long shots are used more often in films, and close shots are used more often in television. Why do you think this is so?

**b.** *Lighting*
This affects the mood and atmosphere of a scene.

*a* Very long shot

*b* Long shot

*c* Medium shot

*d* Close shot

*e* Very close shot
*Source 2.10*

## Source 2.11

1. Where is the source of lighting in these two shots?
2. How does the lighting affect your interpretation of the pictures?

### c. *Focus*

If only part of a picture is in focus, it draws our attention to its importance. How sharp or soft the focus is may also have an affect. Look at the picture adverts on page 65. Why is the focusing softer for the feminine perfume?

### d. *Angle*

Camera shots are often from eye-level angle. This helps to make the viewing seem more natural and life like. High angle shots tend to reduce the importance of a subject, whereas low angle shots may increase the sense of power or authority of a subject. Low angle shots are more often used in film than television.

### e. *Camera movement*

Choices here include:

| | | |
|---|---|---|
| A pan | = | moving the camera from side to side. |
| A tilt | = | moving the camera up or down. |
| A zoom | = | changing the lens to move closer to, or further away from, a subject. |
| A track | = | moving the camera (on wheels) forwards or backwards. |

### Activity

You can see these visual codes in most films and television programmes. From two minutes of recorded fictional television, describe the choice of shot distance, lighting, focus, angle and camera movement. Try to suggest reasons for the various choices.

*Source 2.11*

**f.** *Sound*

Words anchor the meaning of images in film and television as well as photographs. These may be spoken by the subjects appearing in the film, or a voice-over commentary. Music and sound effects also add meaning (see the earlier section on radio).

**g.** *Editing*

Editing involves deciding which shots to use. If the pictures are live, the director has to select the camera position to use at that moment. If it is a recorded programme, the choice will be what to include or leave out, and how the shots should be linked. Linking shots can be done in several ways:

**Straight cut:** changing immediately from one shot to another (the most commonly used link).

**Fade:** making the picture slowly appear or disappear (to represent the beginning or end of a sequence of shots).

**Wipe:** one image removes another.

**Dissolve:** one image slowly emerges to replace the existing image (so for a moment you can see both images).

In addition, there are **special effects**. These include freeze frame, slow motion, split screen (showing more than one picture at the same time), image overlay (placing one picture over another) and computer graphics. Many of these special effects may be seen in pop videos.

***Figure 2.1*** A modern television control room

So mild you can wash your hair as often as you like.

As mild as only nature can be – Timotei shampoo. Timotei is mild both to your hair and to your scalp. It cleans your hair gently, leaving it soft and shiny with a fresh smell of summer meadows.

**Timotei Shampoo.**

PRODUCT INFORMATION - Timotei shampoo has been shown in scientific tests to be mild both to skin and hair. The pH value, about 6, is close to that of normal skin. Contains natural herb extracts.

An engaging way to make a month's salary last a lifetime.

For further information on Diamond Engagement Rings, write to Diamond Information Centre, Dept. E12, 11 Saffron Hill, London EC1N 8RA.

*Source 2.12*

## 5. Advertising codes

Adverts draw on several codes including photography and written language. Therefore, decoding adverts (i.e. interpreting their meanings) requires analysis of a range of: images, signifiers, words, sounds, etc.

### Source 2.12

What qualities of the product are being signified by the images and words in each of the adverts?

**Activity**

Collect four adverts for a similar type of product, e.g. perfume, motor cars, cigarettes etc., and describe how the images and the words (the signifiers) supply meanings about each product. Remember that colour is often an important part of the coding.

### Narrative

Shots are linked in film and television in order to tell a story. The process of producing a story is referred to as **narrative**. This can be divided into two parts: the **plot**, i.e. what happens, and the **discourse** or narration, i.e. how the story is told.

We think in terms of stories all the time. What happened today? What will happen next? These questions are posed in our everyday conversations, or in our fantasies. They might be answered in our diaries or letters. The media are also very much involved in story telling. For centuries, the novel and song have been popular forms of narrative.

*Narrative in pop songs*

On the whole, pop songs are about expressing emotion, often reflecting on love and romance – first meetings, being in love, breaking up, painful memories, etc. Sometimes, borrowing from the folk music tradition, songs may tell a story or provide a social or political message.

***Source 2.13***   *All cried out*

1. Who is telling the story?
2. Why is the chorus important?
3. How might the music and singing add to the story telling?

**Activity**

From your own music collection, listen to 10 songs and describe the main narrative themes.

---

**All Cried Out**

You took your time to come back this time
The grass has grown under your feet
In your absence I changed my mind
And someone else is sitting in your seat

I know that I said there'd be no-one else
I know that I said I'd be true
But baby – I burned cupid's arrow
And here's the short and narrow
I've nothing left to offer you

'Cause I'm all cried out
You took a whole lot of loving for a handful of nothing
All cried out
It's hard to give you something when
You're pushing and shoving me around

So don't look surprised there was no disguise
You knew where I stood from the start
So stop – look around you
You're right back where I found you
Take back your cold and empty heart

You go your way
I'll go mine
I won't stay around here
Don't you waste your time

Lyrics and music by Tony Swain and Steve Jolley
© 1984 J & S Music Ltd.

***Source 2.13***   *(Alison Moyet, All Cried Out, CBS, 1984)*

*Source 2.14*

In narrative, much can be left to the imagination as to what has, or will, happen. This applies even to single images which freeze a moment in time.

***Source 2.14***
What do you think might have happened before and after this photograph was taken?

Holiday pictures are a good example of devices for producing narrative. They often trigger stories of events that led up to, or followed, the subject of the picture.

***Source 2.15***
1. What story is suggested in this advert (the plot)?
2. How is it narrated (the discourse)?
3. Adverts have sometimes been likened to fairy tales. Why is this?

*Source 2.15*

*Photostory narrative*

### Source 2.16
Write a set of captions that could go in the empty bubbles so that the sequence of pictures tells a story. Compare your version with others.

**Activity**

Look at ten further photostories from teenage magazines, and make a list of the main plots, and how the stories are developed (e.g. a problem arises and is eventually solved). Are there any similarities between the stories?

### Television narrative

Stories are obviously central to much of television like soap opera or detective stories. Even where there may be no clear story to tell, narrative questions are built into much of television.

### Source 2.17

How far do narrative questions seem to be part of each of the programmes described in the extract from the *TV Times* (page 26)?

### Building narrative in film and television

#### Time

Only with live coverage on television do you get real time shown. Even then, the real flow of events is often interrupted, as in sport, where **action replays** are often used. In telling a story, editing enables jumps in time to be made. A simple **cut** may move on the story, or possibly lead the viewer back in time (via a flashback). **Fade-outs** or **dissolves** could mean a longer period of time passing. In many Hollywood films, passing time was represented by calendar pages being ripped off or the hands of a clock moving round. The faster the cutting, the greater the opportunity to speed up the story.

#### Point of view

When watching a film or television programme, the viewer is placed in a particular position from which to see the events. A common starting point is the **long shot** which sets the general scene. Closer shots place the viewer in a more personal relationship with the subjects, especially when seen at eye-level view. The viewer may then be drawn in to see the story from the point of view of the participants.

# SATURDAY

## ITV

### LWT

#### 1.05pm
#### Saint & Greavsie

Ian St John and Jimmy Geaves look back at the week's big international games involving England, Scotland and Wales and preview tomorrow's *Big Match Live* between Man Utd and Liverpool.

PRODUCTION TEAM
JIM RAMSAY, JAMIE OAKFORD, CHRIS RHYS
PRODUCER BOB PATIENCE
DIRECTOR JOHN SCRIMINGER
*Independent Television Sport Production*

#### 1.35pm
#### Wrestling

from Huddersfield Town Hall

**Eight Man Battle Royal Special:** Non-stop action is guaranteed in a four-bout programme. First the individual contests — three rounds each, one fall to decide. Then the ultimate show as all eight men attempt to throw each other out of the ring. The last man left standing is the winner. There are one or two familiar faces like British champion Alan Kilby, Yorkshire's King Ben and American globetrotter Ted Heath, but a few new ones too. The weight limit is 15 stone but it still adds up to a lot of manpower and muscle.

COMMENTATOR
KENT WALTON
DIRECTOR GEOFF HALL
PRODUCER
MICHAELE ARCHER
*ITV Production*

#### 2.15pm
#### Comedy Classic: The Cuckoo Waltz

BY GEOFFREY LANCASHIRE
DIANE KEEN
DAVID ROPER
IAN SAYNOR

Has the Hawthornes' new lodger, Adrian Lockett, fallen in love with Fliss? Husband Chris laughs at the idea — at first! ‡

Fliss Hawthorne   Diane Keen
Chris Hawthorne
                         David Roper
Adrian Lockett   Ian Saynor
Connie Wagstaffe
                         Clare Kelly
Holly Galinsky   Rula Lenska
Commère         Dorina Brown
DESIGNER COLIN REES
DIRECTOR DOUGLAS ARGENT
PRODUCER JOHN G TEMPLE
*Granada Television Production*

#### 2.45pm
#### Ice Skating

**TUBORG BRITISH ICE DANCE CHAMPIONSHIPS**

The splendid new ice rink at Bracknell is the venue for the 1987 British Ice Dance Championships. The defending title holders Sharon Jones and Paul Askham are in top form having taken the silver medal in the St Ivel International in October. Can they make it three wins in a row? Tough opposition is expected to come from Britain's number two couple Elizabeth Coates and Alan Abretti. Live and exclusive coverage is introduced by Nick Owen. Commentators are Simon Reed with Betty Callaway and Nicky Slater.

PROGRAMME EDITOR
BRYAN TREMBLE
PRODUCER DOUG HAMMOND
EDITOR PHIL KING
*Independent Television Sport Production*

‡ *indicates Repeat*

#### 4.45pm
#### Results Service

Elton Welsby presents today's sports results.

*Oracle Sports Headlines throughout the week, page 130*

#### 5.00pm
#### ITN News

#### 5.05pm
#### Walt Disney Presents

**DOG WATCH**

Fun and games for navy dog Pluto when he is left on guard aboard his ship.

#### 5.15pm
#### Blockbusters

BOB HOLNESS

The fast-moving general knowledge game show in which 16- to 18-year-olds test their speed and brains on the *Blockbusters* board. Produced in association with Mark Goodson and Talbot Television Ltd.

DIRECTORS JENNY DODD, RICHARD BRADLEY, TERRY STEEL
PRODUCER JENNY DODD
EXECUTIVE PRODUCER TONY WOLFE
*Central Production*

#### 5.45pm
#### 3-2-1

TED ROGERS
PETER BECKETT
KIT AND THE WIDOW
GORDON SCOTT
ADRIAN WALSH
STAN BOARDMAN
Lynda Lee Lewis
The Brian Rogers Connection

Stan Boardman joins Ted Rogers in your big Saturday night entertainment where one lucky couple could go away with £1600. In the newcomer spot is rock singer Peter Beckett, with comedy from Kit and the Widow and Adrian Walsh, and music from multi-instrumentalist Gordon Scott. Don't forget the viewers' competition — see coupon on this page. Writers are Eric Davidson and Wally Malston.

*See page 93*

*Oracle subtitles page 888*

EXECUTIVE PRODUCER
ALAN TARRANT
PRODUCER/DIRECTOR
PATRICIA PEARSON
*Yorkshire Television Production*

#### 6.45pm
#### Copy Cats

AIDEN J HARVEY
ALLAN STEWART
ANDREW O'CONNOR
HILARY O'NEIL
MIKE OSMAN
PAULINE HANNAH
MARK WALKER

More pussyfooting around as those manic *Copy Cats* get their claws into more impressions. The 'Star Trek' team find themselves earthbound on a special mission to destroy an insidious motorway menace. 'Saint & Greavsie' cook up something gruesome and 'Victoria Wood' reveals the inspiration of her songs. Writers are Charlie Adams, Terry Ravenscroft, Alan Wightman, Andrew O'Connor, Bob Phillips, Joe Griffiths, Peter Hickey and John Palmer.

Double act, Chas 'n' Dave — or is it? Could it be Allan Stewart and Aiden J Harvey? Watch 'Copy Cats', 6.45pm.

Comedian Stan Boardman (left) and instrumentalist Gordon Scott add mirth and music to '3-2-1'. See 5.45pm.

Script associate is Charlie Adams.

*See page 29*

DESIGNERS MIKE OXLEY, RICHARD DUNN
EXECUTIVE PRODUCER JOHN AMMONDS
PRODUCER/DIRECTOR VIC FINCH
*LWT Production*

#### 7.15pm
#### Blind Date

CILLA BLACK

More Blind Dates under the watchful eye of Cilla Black. Will it be love, war or simply indifference? Find out each week as girl meets boy and boy meets girl.

*Oracle subtitles page 888*

DESIGNER RICHARD DUNN
ASSOCIATE PRODUCER KEVIN ROAST
DIRECTOR TERRY KINANE
PRODUCER
GILL STRIBLING-WRIGHT
*LWT Production*

#### 8.00pm
#### Home to Roost

BY ERIC CHAPPELL
JOHN THAW
REECE DINSDALE
with JOAN BLACKHAM
LYSETTE ANTHONY

**THE REAL THING**

Why is Matthew tingling in the morning? Henry gives him the benefit of his experience on women.

*Oracle subtitles page 888*

Henry Willows     John Thaw
Matthew Willows
                       Reece Dinsdale
Fiona Fennell   Joan Blackham
Lucy             Lysette Anthony
DESIGNER AGNES HALL
PRODUCER/DIRECTOR
DAVID REYNOLDS
*Yorkshire Television Production*

#### 8.30pm
#### Murder, Mystery, Suspense: Who Killed Miss USA?

DENNIS WEAVER

**FILM** Western marshal Sam McCloud is assigned to take a prisoner, James Waldron, to New York as a witness in the trial of a Puerto Rican who's accused of murdering a beauty queen. When their plane lands in New York, Waldron is kidnapped.

*See film guide, beginning page 53*

*Oracle subtitles page 888*

McCloud       Dennis Weaver
Whitman        Craig Stevens
Peter B Clifford
                      Mark Richman
Chris           Diana Muldaur
Sgt Broadhurst  Terry Carter
Peralta          Mario Alcalde
Fr Nieves           Raul Julia
Waldron          Shelly Novak
Adrienne        Julie Newmar
Billy            Michael Bow
Ramos            Nefti Millet
Mern Ann        Kathy Stritch
Guard         Albert Popwell
First deputy   Gregory Sierra
Second deputy   Tony Dante
Vejar           Ron Henriquez
Chico         Roberto Vargas
TELEPLAY
STANFORD WHITMORE,
RICHARD LEVINSON,
WILLIAM LINK
DIRECTOR RICHARD A COLLA

#### 10.15pm
#### ITN News and Sport

## COUNT ON PRIZE FUN AND WIN A TELLY

Be a winner at home with *3-2-1*. Simply watch tonight's fun-packed programme and listen out for Ted Rogers to announce the special *TVTimes 3-2-1* viewer's question. Answer it correctly and you could win a first prize of a super Hitachi 14in portable colour TV with remote control. There are three ceramic Dusty Bins for runners-up, too. Write the answer on the coupon with your name and address and send it to: *TVTimes 3-2-1* Competition Week 11, Yorkshire Television, Television Centre, Leeds LS3 1JS, to arrive not later than first post on Wednesday 18 November 1987. The first correct entry examined after this date will win the TV. The next three correct will each win a Dusty Bin.

Winners' names will be announced at the end of *3-2-1* on Saturday 21 November. Normal *TVTimes* rules apply.

---

**To TVTimes 3-2-1 Competition Week 11, Yorkshire TV, Television Centre, Leeds LS3 1JS**

The answer to the *3-2-1* viewers' question

week 11 is.......................................

Name.................................................

Address...............................................

..............................Postcode...........

**Closing date 18 November 1987**
BLOCK LETTERS PLEASE

*Source 2.17*

***Source 2.18*** **Visual flow**
Describe what kind of story is
developing here. How is the
narrative developed in each shot?

*The storyboard*
This is the visual illustration or
picture guide to how a story
develops. It is much like a cartoon
comic strip, except there are
added details of how the camera is
to be used to help develop the
story. Below is an example of a
simple storyboard.

For further discussion on
constructing storyboards see
pages 137–8.

***Source 2.18*** Visual flow
(Roland Lewis, *The Video Maker's
Handbook,* Pan, 1987)

### Dodge City Storyboard

**1. LONG SHOT** EXTERIOR.
MAIN STREET, DODGE CITY
WE SEE A HOT, DUSTY WEST-
ERN STREET. TWO MEN FACE
EACH OTHER. THEY ARE NOW
SOME DISTANCE APART.

**2. FULL SHOT** SHERIFF JIM
KINCAID
JIM IS WEARING A WHITE HAT.
HE HAS A GRIM EXPRESSION
ON HIS FACE. AND A SHINY
5-POINT STAR ON HIS LAPEL.

**3. FULL SHOT** — EVIL RANCE
DEVLIN
COMING TOWARD THE SHER-
IFF IS EVIL RANCE DEVLIN.
DRESSED ALL IN BLACK HE IS
CARRYING SIX-GUNS THAT
ARE ALMOST IDENTICAL TO
THOSE THE SHERIFF HAS.
RANCE LOOKS TO HIS LEFT.

**4. INSERT CLOSE UP** A CLOCK
FACE
WE SEE IT'S HIGH NOON

**5. CLOSE UP** — KINCAID'S
FACE
HE IS ALSO LOOKING AT THE
CLOCK. HE TURNS AND
LOOKS THE OPPOSITE WAY
AT HIS DEPUTY, WHO HAS EN-
TERED THE FRAME AS THE
CAMERA PULLS BACK
SLIGHTLY.
DEPUTY: It's time.
SHERIFF: I know.
DEPUTY: Sure you don't want
some help?
SHERIFF: This is my battle. I've
got to face him alone.

**6. LONG SHOT** — MAIN
STREET, DODGE CITY
WE RETURN TO THE FIRST
SHOT AS WE SEE THE MEN
START TO STRIDE TOWARDS
EACH OTHER.

**7. TRACKING MEDIUM SHOT**
— SHERIFF KINCAID
THE CAMERA TRAVELS WITH
THE SHERIFF AS HE STRIDES
TOWARD THE ENEMY.
SHERIFF: This is it for you,
Devlin. I'm taking care of you
once and for all.

**8. TRACKING MEDIUM SHOT**
— EVIL RANCE DEVLIN
FROM THE OTHER DIREC-
TION COMES RANCE DEVLIN,
WITH A SNARL ON HIS LIPS.
RANCE: We'll just see about
that, Sheriff.

**9. CLOSE UP** — DEVLIN'S
GUNS
WE SEE DEVLIN FINGERING
HIS PEARL-HANDLED
REVOLVER.

***Figure 2.2*** Dodge City storyboard (R. Hirschman, R. Proctor, *How to Shoot Better Video,* Hal Leonard Books)

## Realism

If you ever see old silent films, they often seem rather ridiculous, and certainly not realistic.

### Questions for group discussion

1. Why do old films lack 'realism'?
2. What is meant by 'realism'?
3. Which television programmes seem most 'real' to you?

It may well be that your answer to the second question is something like 'true to life'. Modern television may seem more 'true to life' than old films because audience expectations have changed in line with technological developments such as colour, more sensitive cameras, deeper focus, etc. This implies that it is possible to achieve a pure reflection of reality, a true 'window on the world'.

However, television, film and even radio, are only realistic in so far as we are not conscious that they have been put together by directors, producers, actors, etc. Various techniques and conventions help to achieve this effect. In television drama, for example, locations or sets fit us into a 'real' world, the characters appear credible, and every detail is made to seem authentic. The actors do not address the camera, for that would admit the existence of a separate audience. The more involved the audience, the more 'real' the experience. That is not to say there is only one kind of television drama. Soap opera, series (i.e. containing self contained episodes), and single plays all produce a different kind of reality, whether it is in *EastEnders, The Bill* or *Minder*. Often, it is only when conventions of realism are broken, either accidentally (as shown on *It'll Be Alright On The Night*) or

deliberately (as in comedy shows like *The Young Ones*) that they are exposed as a construction.

Whereas television fiction is seen to be based on acting, it is 'factual' programmes like news and documentaries that are thought to be most real. News is discussed in the next chapter (on pages 50–2) but what of documentaries?

## Documentaries

A documentary is a programme which aims to present the truth about a subject. The 'truth' can be coded or represented in many different ways.

---

**Activity**

Compare two different documentaries on television (e.g. on politics, science, natural history) by answering the following questions:

1. Where does the information come from, e.g. a presenter, narrator's voice over, interviews with experts, statistics, the public, etc?
2. Are any sound effects or music used?
3. What kind of narrative is there, e.g. is there a puzzle being solved, a story told, a debate between differing views developed, or a straight description of details?

---

The fact that there is no one way of making a documentary suggests that there is no one way of being able to capture the truth about the world. Film and television always involve choices which mean **interpretations** of what is happening.

One style of documentary which some people claim is the closest to being 'real' has been called the **'fly on the wall'** (or cinema vérité) film. Using this

approach documentary series have been made on the police, schools, the armed forces, prisons and even family life.

*Source 2.19* 'Fly on the wall' documentaries

1. Why is it called 'fly on the wall' filming?
2. Do you think people act naturally once they get used to cameras?
3. Very little voice-over commentary is provided to explain things to the viewer. Does this mean the viewer is more able to make up his or her own mind about what is being shown?

# CAN WE BELIEVE THE FLY ON THE WALL?

The 'fly on the wall' or to coin a phrase 'télé verité' school of documentaries grew up in the sixties and seventies, helped greatly by technical improvements. Crews who had once dragged round huge cameras and enough lighting equipment to illuminate Wembley Stadium were given cameras which fitted snugly on one man's shoulder, and which had lenses and film stock capable of picking up images in almost anything short of total darkness . . . Directors dislike the tag 'fly on the wall' which they say makes them appear secretive; they prefer the phrase 'piece of the furniture', which implies something so familiar that it is visible but largely ignored . . .

The cameraman must provide long, uninterrupted tracking shots and capture fast-moving scenes without any chance of a re-take. . . It was the apparently straight-forward nature of the technique which helped persuade Thames Valley to let Graef and Stewart in. Mr Harry Ross, the acting Deputy Chief Constable, says that by showing police work as it really is, they hoped to dispel the most persistent accusation against them: that they are a closed, secretive organisation which hangs together and protects its own . . .

Most directors claim that men subjects, whether policemen, sailors, public school boys or prisoners, tend to become increasingly oblivious as filming goes on, though they never entirely forget that the camera is there. Roger Mills, whose unit made 'Sailor', 'Strangeways' and 'Hospital' among others of the genre, says that it depends on what the person is doing. 'If a fireman is up a ladder talking a suicide down, he obviously isn't speaking to the camera. But if he's chatting in a small room, he is bound to be more conscious.' . . .

It all boils down, as with most forms of journalism, to the director's own honesty and, without being snide, it is fair to say that most BBC directors share an unswerving and enviable belief in their own integrity . . . This integrity gets its toughest test in the editing, and a clue to this is the 'shooting ratio' – the amount of film consumed by the cameras compared to the amount which winds up on the screen. In a conventional documentary this is around 9 or 10 to 1, in 'télé-verité' it is nearer 20 to 1, and 'Police' would have come in at 30 or 40 to 1, if the series had not been lengthened. The key to the finished programme is, of course,which inches the director chooses from the yards available . . .

With hindsight, several of the Thames Valley officers now think they would have preferred a commentary. Those we spoke to did not actually criticise the editing, but they felt that crucial links had been omitted – usually for legal reasons, or because even two crews could not cover all aspects of a complicated case.

This tallies with the experience of Mr Barry Irving, who is the director of studies at the Police Foundation, an independent research body. He spent nine months observing police interrogations for the Royal Commission on Criminal Procedure and reckoned that 'after a few weeks' the offficers became used to his presence and were unaffected by it.

However, he says that 'Police' has to be regarded chiefly as entertainment, since the prime time television excludes serious exploration of the context and setting . . .

**Source 2.19** (*Observer*, 24 Jan. 1982, on the making of 'Police')

# 3 INSTITUTIONS

**Figure 3.1**

**Figure 3.2**

When you switch on television to watch a particular programme, you will have certain expectations: that the programme will start and finish at specific times, that it might contain particular pleasures for you as a viewer, that if you do not enjoy it you will switch channels or turn off, etc. In other words, watching television is an activity about which there are shared ideas, meanings and practices, i.e. it is an **institution**. We see it as a normal part of everyday life, like reading a newspaper, listening to the radio, shopping or going to school.

Without an audience, television would cease to have any point. Likewise, without television production, there would be nothing for audiences to watch. What brings media producers and audiences together, and how is the relationship between them shaped? This is the study of media as an institution.

# Media as industry

Media products can be compared to any other product sold to the public – washing machines, cars, breakfast cereals, etc. The aim is to sell as many units as possible and achieve the greatest profit for the owners.

## 1. Cinema

The Hollywood studios have always been run as businesses. One of the ways of making profit used to be through the actors and actresses the studios employed. If they were packaged as **stars**, then their films were likely to be popular. Stars in the cinema are performers who become more than mere actors in the eyes of the audience. They are thought to possess something extraordinary, beyond everyday normality. Star quality is usually built up by other media (especially the press and magazines), by presenting them as special people. This is often in response to box office success.

### Source 3.1 and 3.2

1. From the top ten list of stars for 1961, can you explain why any of them were so popular with audiences?
2. Identify some of the stars of the 1930s – 1950s whose films are shown on television today. What is it about each star which made them so popular?
3. Are there any stars in today's films whose appearance will ensure a film's popularity? What of those stars of 1981 listed in source 3.2?
4. How far can pop performers like Michael Jackson be considered as stars?

Although television performers may be referred to as stars, e.g. Terry Wogan or Cilla Black, they do not share the same sense of extraordinariness or glamour as film stars. Those appearing on television tend to have a more familiar and cosy relationship with audiences.

From a business point of view, there are many advantages in the star system. The star has features which can be advertised and marketed – a face, a body, a pair of legs, a voice, a certain kind of personality, real or synthetic – and can be typed as the wicked villain, the honest hero, the fatal siren, the sweet young girl, the neurotic woman. The system provides a formula easy to understand and has made the production of movies seem more like just another business. The use of this formula may serve also to protect executives from talent and having to pay too much attention to the quality of a story or of acting. Here is a standardised product which they can understand, which can be advertised and sold, and which not only they, but also banks and exhibitors, regard as insurance for large profits.

***Source 3.1*** (H. Powdermaker, *Hollywood The Dream Factory*, Little Brown, Boston, 1950)

**Activity**

Using film or pop music fan magazines (like *Film Review, Smash Hits*, etc), select an example of a current star performer and describe how s/he is represented. What kind of image is being constructed? Compare this to the representation of a television personality in the *Radio* or *TV Times*, or the entertainment pages of the popular press. What kind of pictures are used? How are they described? What aspects of their private life are discussed?

**Top 10 stars based on poll of American cinema owners**

**1961**
1. Elizabeth Taylor
2. Rock Hudson
3. Doris Day
4. John Wayne
5. Cary Grant
6. Sandra Dee
7. Jerry Lewis
8. William Holden
9. Tony Curtis
10. Elvis Presley

**1981**
1. Burt Reynolds
2. Clint Eastwood
3. Dudley Moore
4. Dolly Parton
5. Jane Fonda
6. Harrison Ford
7. Alan Alda
8. Bo Derek
9. Goldie Hawn
10. Bill Murray

***Source 3.2*** (William Goldman, *Adventures in the Screen Trade*, McDonald, 1984)

## 2. The press

**Source 3.3**  The changing face of the *Daily Star*

1. What are the two sources of profit for the newspapers discussed in the *Campaign* article?
2. How does it seem that the increased sales for the newspapers have been achieved?

*Source 3.3*

---

MEDIA NEWS

# New-look Star pulls in readers

Despite howls of protest and disgust from agencies and journalists alike, the new-look *Star* is pulling in both punters and advertisers.

Sales are said to be up by 50,000-60,000 since Michael Gabbert became editor on 3 August, coinciding with a month-long bingo drive.

"Bookings for the coming months are running 48 per cent up on this time last year," said Mike Moore, Express Newspapers group advertising director, "and yield is up by 18 per cent."

For the first time ever the *Star* this week is going to two 36-pagers in a single week because of the volume of advertising, added Moore. "We've had many new advertisers in retailing and the motor field this year and because we're coming up to the autumn, the demand for space is considerable."

Meanwhile, *Express* managing director Andrew Cameron added that the *Daily Express*, like the *Star*, has put on up to 60,000 sales a day in the last fortnight as a result of its £500,000 home prize promotion.

Even the ailing *Sunday Express* is showing signs of life. "For the first time in many years it has turned the corner and sales are going up," said Cameron. "They are up by between three and five per cent as we're producing a much better product. It's very newsy."

*a* (*Campaign*, 2 Oct. 1987)

---

# Star 'gone to the sewers'

A SHADOW minister said yesterday that he believed Parliament might have to act to clean up the " sewer end of the British press."

Mr Robin Corbett, opposition spokesman on broadcasting, spoke out after London-based journalists on the Star newspaper had voted against the new editorial policies of the paper, which recently linked up with the downmarket Sunday Sport...

Under the deal, announced last week, Sunday Sport's editorial director, Mr Mike Gabbert, has become editor of the Star. United Newspapers, which owns the Star, has taken a 24.8 per cent stake in the Sunday Sport company, Apollo.

Mr Corbett, a former NUJ executive member, said : " Mr Gabbert is plumbing even deeper depths of pornography and filth. The paper is a disgrace to British journalism, and it deserves to fail."

Mr Gabbert said later: " I am afraid Mr Corbett must be out to lunch. We have had a 3.5 per cent rise in circulation in the first four days of the new-look Star, and for the first time in the history of the paper we have a 36-page paper tomorrow

*b* (*The Guardian*, 11 Aug. 1987)

*c* (*Daily Star*, 7 Aug. 1987)

*Advertising and newspapers*

All newspapers depend to some extent on advertising income. Between 20% and 40% of the content of national daily newspapers consists of advertising. This proportion may be as high as 66% of the Sunday supplement magazines. Increasingly, local newspapers are becoming dependent on advertising, as can be seen by the number which are delivered free of charge to houses. These are called freesheets.

*The effect on choice*

**Source 3.4**  Newspaper, class and advertising

1. Why do the 'quality' daily and Sunday newspapers not need to sell so many copies?
2. How do the 'popular' daily and Sunday newspapers gain most of their income?
3. Which readers seem to have the greatest choice of newspapers?

**Figure 3.3**  The changing face of the *Sun*

The original *Sun* newspaper dates from the last century (see **a**). The current *Sun* started as the *Daily Herald* in 1912 (see **b**) as a paper for the Labour movement. After reaching over 2 million circulation in the 1930s, its sales declined to 1.3 million when it was relaunched as the *Sun* in 1964 (see **c**). It continued to decline (to 1 million) until Rupert Murdoch took over in 1969. He introduced the version similar to today (see **d**), which rose a circulation of 4 million within 10 years.

(T. Douglas, *The Complete Guide to Advertising,* Guide, 1985)

| Newspaper | | Social class of readership | Percentage revenue from sales | Percentage revenue from advertising |
|---|---|---|---|---|
| | April-Sept 1987 | | | |
| Sun | 4 021 122 | | | |
| Daily Mirror | 3 130 734 | mainly working and lower middle | | |
| Star | 1 239 699 | Popular | | |
| Daily Mail | 1 794 458 | daily | 73 | 27 |
| Daily Express | 1 675 070 | | | |
| Today | 326 281 | | | |
| | | | | |
| Daily Telegraph | 1 171 291 | | | |
| Guardian | 472 648 | | | |
| Times | 446 790 | Quality | mainly upper middle | |
| Independent | 325 830 | daily | 42 | 58 |
| Financial Times | 299 036 | | | |
| | | | | |
| News of the World | 5 021 366 | | | |
| Sunday Mirror | 3 001 732 | mainly working and lower middle | | |
| Sunday People | 2 905 273 | Popular | | |
| Sunday Express | 2 222 031 | Sunday | 69 | 31 |
| Mail on Sunday | 1 772 381 | | | |
| | | | | |
| Sunday Times | 1 234 398 | | mainly | |
| Observer | 772 532 | Quality | upper | 34 |
| Sunday Telegraph | 732 808 | Sunday | middle | 66 |

**Source 3.4**  *(ABC)*

## 3. Television

Gaining large audiences is also important for television. In the case of ITV, these are needed to attract advertisers from whom ITV receives much of its income.

The highest rates are charged when the audience is greatest. The BBC does not have advertising. Instead, its income is mainly derived from the licence fee charged to every household with a television set.

Why do you think the BBC is concerned with winning as large an audience as ITV for its programmes?

Audiences are measured by **ratings** (see page 104 for a description). These figures, which are published weekly, show which are the most popular television programmes in rank order. In America, they are so important that a series may be cancelled after two or three weeks if its ratings are poor. The way to obtain high ratings is to produce a programme that has broad popular appeal.

**Source 3.5** American television and advertising
1. Why do you think advertisers pay higher rates for reaching groups like young women and teenagers?
2. America has only one national daily newspaper (the others are local/regional). How do you think this affects advertising on television?

A second aspect of attracting more viewers is **scheduling**. This means choosing the running order of programmes to fit certain time slots.

---

**London weekend televison**

**Rate card No 31 effective January 2, 1987 (excl. VAT)**

**SPOT RATES**

**Friday**

| Time | | 10 secs | 20 secs | 30 secs |
|---|---|---|---|---|
| 17.15–18.00 | 1 | £4,000 | £6,400 | £8,000 |
| 18.00–22.30 | 2 | £10,000 | £16,000 | £20,000 |
| 22.30–Close | 3 | £4,000 | £6,400 | £8,000 |
| | | 40 secs | 50 secs | 60 secs |
| 17.15–18.00 | 1 | £10,664 | £13,328 | £14,000 |
| 18.00–22.30 | 2 | £26,660 | £33,320 | £35,000 |
| 22.30–Close | 3 | £10,664 | £13,328 | £14,000 |

**Saturday**

| Time (pm) | | 10 secs | 20 secs | 30 secs |
|---|---|---|---|---|
| up to 17.30 | 1 | £4,000 | £6,400 | £8,000 |
| 17.30–22.30 | 2 | £10,000 | £16,000 | £20,000 |
| 22.30–Close | 3 | £4,000 | £6,400 | £8,000 |
| | | 40 secs | 50 secs | 60 secs |
| up to 17.30 | 1 | £10,664 | £13,328 | £14,000 |
| 17.30–22.30 | 2 | £26,660 | £33,320 | £35,000 |
| 22.30–Close | 3 | £10,664 | £13,328 | £14,000 |

**Sunday**

| Time | | 10 secs | 20 secs | 30 secs |
|---|---|---|---|---|
| up to 19.30 | 1 | £4,000 | £6,400 | £8,000 |
| 19.30–22.30 | 2 | £10,000 | £16,000 | £20,000 |
| 22.30–Close | 3 | £4,000 | £6,400 | £8,000 |
| | | 40 secs | 50 secs | 60 secs |
| up to 19.30 | 1 | £10,664 | £13,328 | £14,000 |
| 19.30–22.30 | 2 | £26,660 | £33,320 | £35,000 |
| 22.30–Close | 3 | £10,664 | £13,328 | £14,000 |

Longer Spots are pro rata to the 60 secs rate
FIXED SPOTS 30% extra of the rate applicable

**Figure 3.4** (British Rates and Data, 1987)

---

**American television and advertising**

In the 'TV market-place' the advertiser 'buys' his viewers at anything between $2¼ per thousand 'unassorted' to $10½ a thousand if they can be refined down to particular categories like young women, teenagers and so on, who can be more valuable in that form to sellers of specific products. The sums involved are vast: the average 30-second prime-time network television announcement costs about $60,000 (the highest cost to date, for commercials during the first television broadcast of the film *Gone With the Wind*, was $130,000); even low-rated spots average about $45,000. In 1977, commercial television had total revenues of $5.9 billion and profits of $1.4 billion (*Broadcast Yearbook*, 1979).

NB: the rates quoted have since risen to over $500,000 for a 30 second spot during the Superbowl football final (the equivalent of our FA Cup Final).

**Source 3.5** (M. Gurevitch *et al.*, *Culture, Society and the Media*, Methuen, 1982)

1. How did Michael Grade improve the BBC's share of the audience?
2. What restrictions are there on which programmes can be scheduled on television? (These are discussed later in the chapter.)

## Activities

1. Examine the BBC and ITV schedules for the week in the *Radio Times* and *TV Times*. Select what you think is a strong BBC and a strong ITV evening's schedule. Suggest reasons for your choice.
2. Imagine you are the controller of television scheduling for an evening between 6.00 and 11.00 p.m. for either ITV or the BBC. Create a schedule of programmes which you think would gain the largest audience. Try to include a varied mixture i.e. avoid bunching together programmes of a similar kind such as soap operas and comedies.

*Programme sales*
Selling programmes to other countries is an increasing source of revenue for television companies. In fact, many television productions are now international (e.g. British-American co-production). This means that greater financial backing can be achieved and the end product can be sold to more than one country.

MEDIA

# MICHAEL GRADE:
## THE FACE OF ITV'S WORST ENEMY

Grade's reputation rests on the BBC1 weekday schedule introduced in February 1985, with its year-round 7pm shows designed to hook the audience after *Crossroads* and *Emmerdale Farm*. On Mondays, Wednesdays and Fridays, *Wogan*; on Tuesdays and Thursdays, *EastEnders*, which had been two years in preparation under Grade's hapless predecessor, Alan Hart.

This line-up was no instant smash. Until August 1985, BBC1 continued to lose ground. Premiering with nine million, *EastEnders* slumped to 5.2 million before *Emmerdale Farm's* layoff prompted soap fans to revisit Albert Square. At Christmas, *EastEnders* hit 15 million, and now, at 7.30pm, gets a steady 13–16 million . . .

Some other breakthroughs were contrived by breaking inherited rules: for instance, Grade moved *Panorama* from 8.10pm to 9.30pm on Mondays, initially improving its ratings but ending non-aggression with Granada's *World in Action* at 8.30pm – BBC1 pitted situation comedy against it . . .

NB: Michael Grade became head of Channel Four in late 1987.

*Source 3.6*   (*Campaign*, Haymarket, 16 Oct. 1987)

## Source 3.7

1. List the different ways in which Thames Television sells its products to gain revenue. Selling a product in more than one form is called **multimarketing** e.g. Thames' *Dangermouse* products.
2. Can you identify any examples of multimarketing in the media other than those included in the source opposite?

### 4. Pop music

Pop music is an ever growing industry. Whilst sales of singles and albums have declined, cassettes and compact discs have grown rapidly. In 1986, the total value of music sales on record, cassette, and compact disc in Britain was officially worth £425 million. Apart from music sales, there are other related sources of profit.

# SELLING THAMES TO THE WORLD

Some 126 countries around the world now watch Thames programmes through the distribution network of Thames Television International, whose enterprise and performance was recognised by The Queen's Award for Export Achievement 1984.

Format sales are an important part of TTI's revenue. The Thames sit-com *Man About The House* became 'Three's Company' in America.

TTI is arguably the most successful and most profitable of the British independent distribution companies, with a strong track record in programme sales and a growing business in ancillary areas such as home video, publishing and merchandising. The record is particularly strong in the USA which now represents more than 65% of the world market for audio-visual products. The Thames symbol is now well-known to American viewers through the syndicated sale of top series like *The World at War*, *Hollywood*, *Crime Inc* and *The Benny Hill Show*. Benny Hill, presented in 1985 with a Montreux Festival Award for the most widely distributed comedy show worldwide, is now seen every week and usually five nights a week on more than 100 US television stations.

Five years ago, Thames Television International joined forces with Methuen General Books to form a joint publishing imprint – Thames/Methuen. The success of Thames Publishing today testifies to the commercial validity of the belief that publications are a necessary companion to responsible broadcasting.

The spirit and content of Thames programmes are now captured by a list of Thames/Methuen titles which embraces the whole range of Thames' output, as well as productions by other television companies,

. . . Thames programme rights are also exploited through the licensing of merchandising rights to manufacturers of toys, games and clothing. A wide range of *Dangermouse* products are available in the UK and plans are underway for a major launch in the United States linked to the syndication sales of the series. Records and cassettes of television music are also regularly released. In 1985, soundtracks for *Reilly – Ace of Spies*, *Prospects*, *Monsignor Quixote* and *L'Enfance du Christ* were all successfully marketed.

Capitalizing on the quality of Thames output, Thames Video licenses a wide range of video-cassettes around the world, achieving significant success with *The World at War* and *The Benny Hill Show* in America.

Thames Video has recently undertaken a venture with major distributors The Video Collection. Ten titles – including *Torvill and Dean*, *The Royal Wedding* and *Alias The Jester* – are to be marketed in main High Street multiples under the label of 'The Thames Collection'.

**Source 3.7** (*Thames Television Annual Report*, 1986)

**Source 3.8**  Selling his soul
In what ways is Michael Jackson selling more than just his music?

The use of videos to promote pop music increased considerably in the 1980s. One television channel in America, MTV (Music Television), is devoted solely to showing such videos. In Britain television programmes like *The Chart Show* rely heavily on pop videos.

1. Are pop videos simply another form of (free) promotional advert?
2. In what ways have television adverts become like pop videos (for example, the Levi Jeans adverts)?

# Selling his soul

The centrepiece of the TV special *Michael Jackson: The Magic Returns* that promoted his new album on CBS television was Jackson's latest video *Bad*, a 17-minute promotional clip directed by Martin Scorsese at a cost of $2 million. Jacko portrays a ghetto boy made good who proves his 'badness' (i.e. street credibility) to his old hoodlum friends by *dancing* . . .

Jackson is a black guy supposedly in touch with the dangerous side of 'the street'; but that link keeps him in touch with the beat, too. And this beat defeats baddies . . .

Perhaps his audience likes to believe that music really *can* defeat the politics of those mean streets.

Like a lot of today's pop stars, Michael Jackson doesn't get out of bed until he can find someone to sponsor him to do so. *Bad's* title track was pre-sold to Pepsi. Halfway through the TV special that promoted it, Pepsi screened one of their ads – featuring Michael Jackson, and the music we'd just heard in the promotional video. His fee for the latest series of Pepsi ads is $15 millions. Thus this 30-minute,

primetime slot simultaneously promoted three products (video, album, cola), from which Jackson can expect multi-million dollar earnings . . .

For Jackson, the media are no mere promotional tool designed to sell another commodity (music). His 15-minute video, *Thriller*, is the highest-selling home video ever. The songs performed in the *Caption Eo* film aren't available on any record – you have to pay to visit Disneyland to hear them . . .

But this success has its price. Almost no one talks about Jackson's *music* any more. *Rolling Stone* has reported that his ambition is to out-sell *Thriller* almost three-fold and shift 100 million copies of the *Bad* LP.

**Source 3.8**  (*The Listener*, 1 Oct. 1987)

## The media and big business

### Concentration of ownership

Fewer and fewer companies control the majority of media production. It has been estimated that in the 1970s in Britain the top five companies in each area of media production accounted for:
71% daily newspaper circulation
74% homes with commercial television
78% cinema admissions
70% paperback sales
65% record sales.
Many of these companies have interests in more than one media, as well as owning other types of company. Such large organisations are called **conglomerates**.

*Source 3.9*
Why should it be of concern that one company (in this case dominated by one man) should control so many different media interests?

---

### Activity

Obtain details of a media conglomerate by writing to the company asking them for their annual report, which is issued free. Plot a chart of all the media owned completely or partly by the company. Such companies include the following:

Thorn EMI, Pearson plc, Reed International, Thompson United Newspapers, Associated Newspapers, Granada and Maxwell Communications.

---

### How much control?

It is possible to exaggerate the influence that big business interests have on the media.

---

NEWS INTERNATIONAL
(owned by Rupert Murdoch)

**Media interests**

Newspapers:
*Sun, The Times, Today, The Sunday Times, News of the World* (Britain); *New York Post, Chicago Sun-Times*, etc. (USA); *Daily Sun, Herald* and *Weekly Times* (Australia).

Television:
*Fox* TV Network (USA)
*Channel 10* (Australia)
*Sky Channel* (Satellite)

Books:
*Fontana*

**Other Interests**
Transport, oil, gas

*Source 3.9*

---

*The case of pop music*

***Source 3.10*** The independents

***Source 3.11*** Pop vs. independent charts
1. What are the main reasons for the growth of independent record companies?
2. How far can they challenge the major record companies?
3. Compare the mainstream and independent charts. How do they differ in terms of music?

---

### The independents

There has been a rapid growth in small independent record publishing companies with their own marketing labels – some 150 are now in operation in the UK . . . some of these independents (or 'indies' as they are called) emerged from existing independent recording studios (mostly small or medium sized) who decided to set up their own labels, to handle groups who they felt had a future but whom the majors would not handle. Some groups have also set up their own companies . . . Although they all obviously had commercial motives, they were equally concerned with making a new type of music – and a new type of production system – more widely available.

Many independents operated very much at the fringe, often producing their own records using secondhand machines. Cheap floppy discs, used by the majors for promotion, were sometimes used. Distribution was also much less conventional, e.g. at concerts or other gigs and via underground and progressive bookshops and record sales outlets . . . The advent of cheaper studio recording equipment has made it possible for independents to flourish. A modern semi-professional console (mixer) can cost as little as £600 and yet be technically equivalent to the sort of equipment that the majors were using in the 1960s, with studio and running costs down to as little as £4 per hour (compared to say £75 per hour in conventional large studios). A typical record can therefore be put out at a cost of as little as £200 or less . . . But such records only rarely make the charts – records produced in professional, quality sound recording environments are still usually the most successful in sales terms . . . The main stumbling block for the independents so far – apart from distribution – is the fact that, although they can produce master tapes in cheap studios, these still have to be farmed out to conventional disc cutting and pressing firms . . .

*Source 3.10* (*Science, Technology and Popular Culture*, Open University, 1982)

# TOP 50 NETWORK SINGLES

| | | | |
|---|---|---|---|
| 1 | (1) | THE ONLY WAY IS UP | Yazz & The Plastic Population/Big Life |
| 2 | (2) | THE LOCOMOTION | Kylie Minogue/PWL |
| 3 | (3) | I NEED YOU | B.V.S.M.P./Debut |
| 4 | (6) | THE EVIL THAT MEN DO | Iron Maiden/EMI |
| 5 | (4) | SUPERFLY GUY | S'Express/Rhythm King |
| 6 | (8) | FIND MY LOVE | Fairground Attraction/RCA |
| 7 | (22) | HANDS TO HEAVEN | Breathe/Siren |
| 8 | (7) | YOU CAME | Kim Wilde/MCA |
| 9 | (9) | REACH OUT I'LL BE THERE | Four Tops/Motown |
| 10 | (5) | NOTHING'S GONNA CHANGE MY LOVE FOR YOU | Glen Medeiros/London |
| 11 | (10) | HUSTLE TO THE MUSIC | Funky Worm/Fon |
| 12 | (16) | MARTHA'S HARBOUR | All About Eve/Mercury |
| 13 | (24) | GOOD TRADITION | Tanita Tikaram/WEA |
| 14 | (41) | MY LOVE | Julio Iglesias featuring Stevie Wonder/CBS |
| 15 | (-) | PUSH IT/TRAMP | Salt 'N' Pepa/London/Champion |
| 16 | (31) | THE HARDER I TRY | Brother Beyond/EMI |
| 17 | (20) | LIKE DREAMERS DO | Mica Paris featuring Courtney Pine/4th & Broadway |
| 18 | (18) | I SAY NOTHING | Voice Of The Beehive/London |
| 19 | (13) | I WANT YOUR LOVE | Transvision Vamp/MCA |
| 20 | (12) | I DON'T WANT TO TALK ABOUT IT | Everything But The Girl/blanco y negro |
| 21 | (26) | HAPPY EVER AFTER | Julia Fordham/Circa |
| 22 | (56) | ON THE BEACH SUMMER '88 | Chris Rea/WEA |
| 23 | (14) | ROSES ARE RED | Mac Band/MCA |
| 24 | (21) | ALL FIRED UP | Pat Benatar/Chrysalis |
| 25 | (15) | PEEK A BOO | Siouxsie & The Banshees/Wonderland |
| 26 | (35) | WORKING IN A GOLDMINE | Aztec Camera/WEA |
| 27 | (34) | ROCK MY WORLD | Five Star/Tent |
| 28 | (17) | DIRTY DIANA | Michael Jackson/Epic |
| 29 | (44) | WHEN IT'S LOVE | Van Halen/Warner Bros |
| 30 | (63) | RUSH HOUR | Jane Wiedlin/EMI Manhattan |
| 31 | (37) | SOMEWHERE DOWN THE CRAZY RIVER | Robbie Robertson/Geffen |
| 32 | (19) | FOOLISH BEAT | Debbie Gibson/Atlantic |
| 33 | (-) | KING OF EMOTION | Big Country/Mercury |
| 34 | (47) | YE KE KE KE | Mory Kante/London |
| 35 | (62) | SOLDIER OF LOVE | Donny Osmond/Virgin |
| 36 | (23) | LOVE BITES | Def Leppard/Bludgeon Riffola |
| 37 | (-) | SWEET CHILD O' MINE | Guns 'N' Roses/Geffen |
| 38 | (40) | CHOCOLATE GIRL | Deacon Blue/CBS |
| 39 | (27) | THE TWIST (YO TWIST) | Fat Boys & Chubby Checker/Urban |
| 40 | (45) | CATCH MY FALL | Billy Idol/Chrysalis |
| 41 | (36) | WAP-BAM-BOOGIE/DON'T BLAME IT ON THAT GIRL | Matt Bianco/WEA |
| 42 | (52) | DON'T BE CRUEL | Bobby Brown/MCA |
| 43 | (38) | JIBARO | Electra/London |
| 44 | (-) | I WON'T BLEED FOR YOU | Climie Fisher/EMI |
| 45 | (61) | TEARDROPS | Womack & Womack/4th & Broadway |
| 46 | (25) | WHAT CAN I SAY TO MAKE YOU LOVE ME | Alexander O'Neal/Tabu |
| 47 | (53) | ANYTHING FOR YOU | Gloria Estefan & The Miami Sound Machine/Epic |
| 48 | (72) | BLIND | Talking Heads/EMI |
| 49 | (30) | FAST CAR | Tracy Chapman/Elektra |
| 50 | (68) | LOVE IS THE GUN | Blue Mercedes/MCA |

COMPILED BY MRIB

# TOP 30 ALBUMS

| | | | |
|---|---|---|---|
| 1 | (1) | NOW THAT'S WHAT I CALL MUSIC 12 | Various Artists/EMI/Virgin/Polygram |
| 2 | (4) | KYLIE | Kylie Minogue/PWL |
| 3 | (3) | TRACY CHAPMAN | Tracy Chapman/Elektra |
| 4 | (5) | IDOL SONGS – 11 OF THE BEST | Billy Idol/Chrysalis |
| 5 | (2) | THE HITS ALBUM/TAPE 8 | Various Artists/CBS/WEA/BMG |
| 6 | (7) | THE FIRST OF A MILLION KISSES | Fairground Attraction/RCA |
| 7 | (6) | BAD | Michael Jackson/Epic |
| 8 | (12) | THE GREATEST EVER ROCK 'N' ROLL MIX | Various Artists/Stylus |
| 9 | (9) | TANGO IN THE NIGHT | Fleetwood Mac/Warner Bros |
| 10 | (-) | THE BEST OF THE EAGLES | The Eagles/Asylum |
| 11 | (8) | PUSH | Bros/CBS |
| 12 | (30) | RAINTOWN/RICHES | Deacon Blue/CBS |
| 13 | (11) | DIRTY DANCING | Soundtrack/RCA |
| 14 | (10) | THE COLLECTION | Barry White/Mercury |
| 15 | (13) | SMALL WORLD | Huey Lewis & The News/Chrysalis |
| 16 | (18) | IDLEWILD | Everything But The Girl/blanco y negro |
| 17 | (14) | LOVESEXY | Prince/Paisley Park |
| 18 | (15) | POPPED IN SOULED OUT | Wet Wet Wet/Precious Organisation |
| 19 | (20) | LOVE | Aztec Camera/Warner Bros |
| 20 | (17) | KICK | INXS/Mercury |
| 21 | (19) | WIDE AWAKE IN DREAMLAND | Pat Benatar/Chrysalis |
| 22 | (22) | WHITNEY | Whitney Houston/Arista |
| 23 | (24) | HEAVEN ON EARTH | Belinda Carlisle/Virgin |
| 24 | (24) | HEARSAY | Alexander O'Neal/Tabu |
| 25 | (31) | HYSTERIA | Def Leppard/Bludgeon Riffola |
| 26 | (34) | JULIA FORDHAM | Julia Fordham/Circa |
| 27 | (21) | A SALT WITH A DEADLY PEPA | Salt 'N' Pepper/London |
| 28 | (16) | THRILLER | Michael Jackson/Epic |
| 29 | (44) | LET IT BEE | Voice Of The Beehive/London |
| 30 | (33) | ROLL WITH IT | Steve Winwood/Virgin |

COMPILED BY MRIB

BIG COUNTRY GET EMOTIONAL

HOUSE OF LOVE DESTROY THE HEART

DEACON BLUE GET RICH IN RAINTOWN

# INDIE SINGLES

| | | | |
|---|---|---|---|
| 1 | (1) | THE ONLY WAY IS UP | Yazz & The Plastic Population/Big Life |
| 2 | (2) | THE LOCOMOTION | Kylie Minogue/PWL |
| 3 | (3) | SUPERFLY GUY | S'Express/Rhythm King |
| 4 | (-) | DESTROY THE HEART | House of Love/Creation |
| 5 | (4) | DEF CON ONE | Pop Will Eat Itself/Chapter 22 |
| 6 | (6) | UNBEARABLE | The Wonderstuff/Far Out Recording Co |
| 7 | (12) | CHRISTINE | House of Love/Creation |
| 8 | (-) | YOU MADE ME REALISE | My Bloody Valentine/Creation |
| 9 | (7) | SMASH CLAUSE 28 | Chumbawumba/Agitprop |
| 10 | (5) | SOMETHING NICE | Robert Lloyd & The New Four Seasons/In Tape |
| 11 | (10) | ALWAYS THE LIGHT | Weather Prophets/Creation |
| 12 | (11) | THE MERCY SEAT | Nick Cave & The Bad Seeds/Mute |
| 13 | (20) | KEEP THE CIRCLE | Inspiral Carpets/Playtime |
| 14 | (-) | SUNSHINE SUPERMAN | Salvation/Karbon |
| 15 | (10) | GOODBYE JIMMY DEAN | Boys Wonder/Boys Wonder |
| 16 | (18) | TESTCARD | Ta'ulah Gosh/53rd & 3rd |
| 17 | (8) | ATMOSPHERE | Joy Division/Factory |
| 18 | (16) | MOONCHILD | Fields Of The Nephilim/Situation Two |
| 19 | (9) | MEET EVERY SITUATION HEAD ON | M.E.S.H./Castalia |
| 20 | (-) | DEAN'S ELEVENTH DREAM | James Dean Driving Experience/Autumn Glow |

COMPILED BY MRIB

# ALBUMS

| | | | |
|---|---|---|---|
| 1 | (-) | DOING IT FOR THE KIDS | Various Artists/Creation |
| 2 | (1) | TOMMY | Wedding Present/Reception |
| 3 | (5) | HOUSE OF LOVE | House of Love/Creation |
| 4 | (3) | KYLIE | Kylie Minogue/PWL |
| 5 | (2) | SUBSTANCE 1977-80 | Joy Division/Factory |
| 6 | (6) | OUT TO LUNCH WITH AHEAD OF OUR TIME | Various Artists/Ahead Of Our Time |
| 7 | (7) | ACID HOUSE VOL 1 | Various Artists/BPM |
| 8 | (4) | SUCK ON THE PASTELS | Pastels/Creation |
| 9 | (10) | TRAIN ABOVE THE CITY | Felt/Creation |
| 10 | (11) | COLORBLIND JAMES EXPERIENCE | Colorblind James Experience/Fundamental |
| 11 | (12) | 69 | AR Kane/Rough Trade |
| 12 | (8) | 4 OF A KIND | DRI/Roadrunner |
| 13 | (18) | REEK OF PURIFICATION | Carcass/Earache |
| 14 | (9) | GEORGE BEST | Wedding Present/Reception |
| 15 | (16) | THE INNOCENTS | Erasure/Mute |
| 16 | (15) | THE TENDER PERVERT | Momus/Creation |
| 17 | (13) | SONIC DEATH | Sonic Youth/Blast First |
| 18 | (-) | OUT OF THE DARK | Kreator/Noise |
| 19 | (14) | SURVIVE | Nuclear Assault/Under One Flag |
| 20 | (19) | SUBSTANCE 1987 | New Order/Factory |

COMPILED BY MRIB

# US SINGLES

| | | | |
|---|---|---|---|
| 1 | (2) | MONKEY | George Michael/Columbia |
| 2 | (1) | ROLL WITH IT | Steve Winwood/Virgin |
| 3 | (7) | I DON'T WANT TO GO ON WITH YOU | Elton John/MCA |
| 4 | (6) | I DON'T WANNA LIVE WITHOUT YOU | Chicago/Full Moon |
| 5 | (3) | SIGN YOUR NAME | Terence Trent D'Arby/Columbia |
| 6 | (5) | 1-2-3 | Gloria Estefan & Miami Sound Machine/Epic |
| 7 | (8) | LOVE WILL SAVE THE DAY | Whitney Houston/Arista |
| 8 | (11) | PERFECT WORLD | Huey Lewis & The News/Chrysalis |
| 9 | (14) | SWEET CHILD O' MINE | Guns 'N' Roses/Geffen |
| 10 | (12) | FAST CAR | Tracy Chapman/Elektra |

# US AIRPLAY ALBUMS

| | | | |
|---|---|---|---|
| 1 | (2) | ROLL WITH IT | Steve Winwood/Virgin |
| 2 | (1) | OU812 | Van Halen/Warner Bros |
| 3 | (3) | JUST BEFORE THE BULLETS FLY | Gregg Allman Band/Epic |
| 4 | (7) | LET IT ROLL | Little Feat/Warner Bros |
| 5 | (5) | WIDE AWAKE IN DREAMLAND | Pat Benatar/Chrysalis |
| 6 | (4) | HEAVY NOVA | Robert Palmer/EMI Manhattan |
| 7 | (9) | COCKTAIL (SOUNDTRACK) | Various Artists/Elektra |
| 8 | (6) | SMALL WORLD | Huey Lewis & The News/Chrysalis |
| 9 | (8) | APPETITE FOR DESTRUCTION | Guns 'N' Roses/Geffen |
| 10 | (-) | DON'T BE AFRAID OF THE DARK | Robert Cray Band/Mercury |

US charts courtesy of Radio & Records

MELODY MAKER

**Source 3.11** (*Melody Maker*, 20 Aug. 1988)

In the last thirty years, the record industry has regularly failed to predict audience demand. They have been slow to react to new musical developments, such as with the original rock and roll movement, and more recently with the 1970s punk music. To some extent, this is reflected in the relationship between music and radio.

*Rebel radio*

Prior to *Radio 1* starting in 1967, the BBC played only 3–4 hours of pop music a week! In the mid 1960s, pirate radio stations operating offshore were being listened to by up to 2 million listeners. Stations like *Radio Caroline* were simply broadcasting non-stop pop music, with a few adverts to earn revenue. Since 1973, independent local radio (ILR) stations have also been broadcasting.

## How to be a radio pirate

You will need:

**A transmitter,** ideally over 10 watts, but less can be used with a powerful aerial. You can't get one over the counter in Britain, but here are some alternatives:

- Buy one from another pirate. (Beware of rip-offs.)
- Buy one over the counter abroad. For example, in Italy you can buy a high quality 50 watts transmitter for £200. You then have to smuggle it home. You can buy a transmitter from: Nuova Electronica, Via Cracovia 19, Bologna, Italy.
- Build your own. Although a hobbyist could build one, specialist (RF) experience is essential, especially for very tricky tuning. Try to interest radio hams or dissident engineers.

**Test equipment** £250 should equip you with the essentials to test, build and tune a transmitter. These include:
- SWR bridge/power meter
- Frequency counter to 150 MHz
- Multimeter
- 50 Ω dummy load
- Antenna. Adapt a design from the *Two Metre Antenna Handbook* (Babani or Tabs books) or adapt one from an amateur radio handbook. Make it easily collapsible for concealment or for running away.
- Amateur radio handbooks

### How to broadcast

The factor which determines the area covered on FM is the height of placement of the aerial. Site it on a high tower block or a large hill outside the area to be covered. On a 15 storey tower block, 40 watts should reach a 20-mile radius. VHF signals travel in (nearly) straight lines. In very hilly country, or for wider coverage, use medium wave.

In cities, tower blocks are the ideal answer. To get on the roof you need a key. Keys are standardized (for fire risk reasons) and you can get one from firemen, lift engineers, caretakers etc., or from another pirate. Bring with you your transmitter, a roll of co-axial cable (no longer than you need, as you lose power), a cheap cassette player, leads, a fused plug board, a radio for testing, gaffer tape, and aerial. Once on the roof, find the lift room or a heating room with an electric wall socket.

***Figure 3.5*** (J. Hind and S. Mosco, *Rebel Radio*, Pluto, 1985)

**Source 3.12**

1. Why is pirate radio still so common?
2. Which audience needs are being met? It may be possible to tune into a pirate radio station in your area if you live near a large city, especially London. (NB: It is illegal to listen to such stations.)

# Pirates who storm the open airwaves

**Martin Wroe** looks at illegal radio stations hoping to become legitimate broadcasters

LAST WEEK Radio 1 was given a rude warning. The BBC's most popular radio station was beaten into third place in a London listeners' poll not merely by Capital Radio, the powerful independent station, but by Kiss FM, an illegal, weekends-only pirate radio dance music station catering for radical young people of all races.

Gordon Mac, the 27-year-old north London entrepreneur who controls Kiss FM, competes with the likes of LWR, Time, Fresh FM and Solar for a growing audience of pirate radio listeners in the capital. The station is one of about 90 land-based illegal broadcasters, 40 of which serve London.

Every time Kiss FM takes to the air (on an unoccupied frequency) officers of the Department of Trade and Industry fly at its heels. In the last two years, Mr Mac has had equipment confiscated more than 100 times. During 1987, 200 DTI officials made 377 raids on 79 different pirates.

Kiss FM is the most popular on the capital's "alternative" funky club circuit: the station is closely bound up with promoting club-world. A Haringey record shop acts as a mail-box for the station.

BRIAN SHUEL

Gordon Mac with DJ Norman Jay at Kiss FM's secret studio. Egg boxes on the walls improve sound quality

**Source 3.12**  (*The Independent*, 13 Jan. 1988)

### Independents

The ability to set up independent media production partly depends on the cost of the technology required. Apart from records and radio, small-scale independent publishing has always been popular, e.g. fanzines, political interests, community groups, etc. More recently, independent video production has grown. There are even pirate television stations broadcasting.

### Supply and demand

The large corporations depend on selling their products to the public to earn their profits. Judging from the success of some small independent media productions, the bigger companies do not completely control the market.

*Figure 3.6*

***Source 3.13*** Studio executives

1. Why do you think making media products is an especially risky business?
2. Why might the risks of failing to please the public be greater in some media more than others?

Nobody has total freedom in media production not least because of regulation by the law and the government.

---

**Studio Executives**

Studio executives are intelligent, brutally overworked men and women who share one thing in common with baseball managers: They wake up every morning of the world with the knowledge that sooner or later they're going to get fired . . .

They are responsible for what gets up there on the silver screen. Compounding their problem of no job security in the decision-making process is the single most important fact, perhaps, of the entire movie industry:

NOBODY KNOWS ANYTHING.

Not one person in the entire motion picture field *knows* for a certainty what's going to work. Every time out it's a guess – and, if you're lucky, an educated one . . .

*Raiders* is the number-four film in history as this is being written. I don't remember any movie that had such power going in. It was more or less the brainchild of George Lucas and was directed by Steven Spielberg, the two unquestioned wunderkinder [wonder boys] of show business

(*Star Wars, Jaws,* etc.). Probably you all knew that. But did you know that *Raiders of the Lost Ark* was offered to every single studio in town – *and they all turned it down*?

All except Paramount.

Why did Paramount say yes? Because nobody knows anything. And why did all the other studios say no? Because nobody knows anything. And why did Universal, the mightiest studio of all, pass on *Star Wars*, a decision that just may cost them, when all the sequels and spinoffs and toy money and book money and video-game money are totalled, over a *billion* dollars? Because nobody, *nobody* – not now, not ever – knows the least goddam thing about what is or isn't going to work at the box office . . .

And they had passed on *E.T.*

Columbia had had it, developed it for a million dollars, took a survey, and discovered the audience for the movie would be too limited to make it profitable. So they let it go. (Universal picked it up and may make back the billion they didn't earn by dropping *Star Wars*.) . . .

***Source 3.13*** (William Goldman, *Adventures in the Screen Trade*, McDonald, 1984)

# State control

## General laws applying to the media

Media products are controlled by laws. These include:

**1.** *The Official Secrets Act*
Originally, this was designed to stop secrets going to possible enemies of the state, and the Act was very wide ranging. During 1986–7, BBC programmes on television and radio about the secret services were censored.

Under the proposed new Official Secrets Act, the media may be prosecuted for disclosing information about the security services, defence and the conduct of international relations.

**2.** *Libel*
The libel law exists to protect anyone against unfair or damaging public statements. It is often used against newspapers.

**3.** *Contempt of court*
This prevents the media reporting anything which might affect a fair trial.

**4.** *National emergency*
This mainly applies to war. For example, during the Second World War the Prime Minister, Winston Churchill, banned the *Daily Worker* (a Communist newspaper) for fear it would harm national unity. With the 1982 Falklands War, some government censorship was used. Only officially approved journalists were allowed to travel with the armed forces, and all media reports were vetted by the Ministry of Defence before being made public.

**5.** *Obscene Publications Act*
A very controversial law which has been used mainly in relation to sexually explicit material. There is much pressure to extend controls, especially for sex and violence (see the discussion on violence and the media, pages 120–122).

## Media regulations

*Cinema*
Cinema films, and more recently, videos, are subject to the approval of the British Board of Film Censors before being made available to the public. The Board catagorises films and videos as U, PG, 15 or 18. The main guideline is whether a film or video would 'offend against good taste or decency', and in the case of video, is it 'suitable for viewing in the home'?

*Broadcasting*
To broadcast in Britain requires a licence. Two organisations have had the right to provide television and radio services; the BBC (since 1926) and the Independent Broadcasting Authority, IBA (since 1955). Between them they controlled all national and local television and radio in Britain until the 1980s.

The BBC helped establish the principle that television in Britain should provide more than just entertainment, but rather it should operate as a **public service**, meaning information and education should also be important features of what is broadcast. This public service aim is not part of most other countries' television stations.

The BBC and the IBA each have a set of governors appointed by the Home Secretary to ensure that government regulations concerning broadcasting are enforced. The 1981 Broadcasting Act is the basis for current rules and guidelines operated by the governors. Although the BBC has regional centres, it is one company, whose income mainly comes from the licence fee paid by television users – the public. The IBA is more complex.

**Source 3.14** The IBA's functions

1. How many of the 15 ITV companies can you list? The companies can be identified by their logos which appear before the programmes they have made.
2. From the *TV Times*, list the programmes which you think:
   a. ensure entertainment programmes are balanced by factual and educational programmes.
   b. provide interest to viewers in your region.
   c. have been placed later in the evening in line with IBA's family viewing policy.
   d. appeal to minority interests on Channel 4.

Basing its policy on the Broadcasting Act 1981, the IBA is both a 'regulator' and a 'publisher'. It has four main functions:

### 1. SELECTION AND APPOINTMENT OF THE PROGRAMME COMPANIES

Fifteen separate companies are under fixed-term contracts with the IBA to provide the ITV programme service in 14 areas (London being served by two companies: one for weekdays, one for weekends). Each company is required to produce programmes of particular interest to viewers in its area. The ITV companies serving Northern Ireland, Scotland and Wales need also to reflect their distinct regional character and culture...

### 2. SUPERVISION OF THE PROGRAMME PLANNING

Although the IBA does not itself make programmes, it is ultimately answerable to Parliament and the public for everything it transmits. The Broadcasting Act requires the IBA to ensure that the programmes provide a proper balance of information, education and entertainment; a high general standard in all respects; and, so far as possible, accuracy in news, due impartiality in matters of political and industrial controversy, and the avoidance of offences to good taste and decency...

In approving the schedules for the television and radio services, the IBA may at any time request additional information about particular programmes, require changes to be made or refuse to transmit any material...

In assessing the draft schedules, the IBA has a number of considerations in mind.

Has a wide range of interests been catered for? Are programmes scheduled at appropriate times of day? Are early evening programmes suitable for all the family? Are there enough regional programmes and programmes for children? Education and religion have always been important elements in Britain's tradition of 'public service' broadcasting; have viewers' interests in these fields been catered for properly? Is there a good balance between entertainment and factual programming, and have some of the more demanding programmes been given a suitable proportion of peak-time viewing? Are programmes of the same sort being 'bunched' together? All these factors are important for the viewer looking for interesting and enjoyable viewing.

Channel 4 has to observe some additional requirements: to appeal to interests and tastes not generally catered for by ITV; to make greater provision for education programmes, and to be more experimental. These all help to give Channel 4 its distinctive character.

### 3. CONTROL OF THE ADVERTISING

The IBA controls all the advertising transmitted on ITV, Channel 4, ILR and Oracle Teletext. It checks that the frequency, amount and nature of the advertisements are in accordance with the law and, in particular, the Broadcasting Act and the extensive rules and principles laid down by the IBA.

...Television advertising is limited to seven minutes an hour, averaged over the day's programmes, with a normal maximum of seven minutes in any 'clock-hour' (e.g. 7 – 8 p.m.). In radio, the advertising is limited, normally, to a maximum of nine minutes in each hour.

### 4. TRANSMISSION OF THE PROGRAMMES

The IBA transmits all the Independent Broadcasting services: it builds, owns and operates the transmitters, allocating them to carry programmes presented by the various programme companies; arranges distribution links and establishes technical standards.

**Source 3.14** (*Television and Radio*, IBA, 1988)

In 1983 a new organisation, the Cable Authority was set up to regulate cable television, and grant licences to local stations to broadcast. The IBA awarded the first three channels for Direct Broadcast Satellite (DBS) to BSB in 1988. Other television stations broadcasting via satellite to Britain are unregulated as they are operating from outside our national boundaries (for a further discussion of new technology see pages 57–61).

In 1988 the government set out proposals for broadcasting in the 1990s which included setting up a new television organisation, the Independent Television Commission, to replace both the IBA and the Cable Authority. It will be responsible for ITV (Channel 3), Channel 4, cable TV, as well as a new national channel (channel 5), and will apply 'lighter' programme requirements than in the past, meaning a higher proportion of programmes may be entertainment rather than say educational or religious in emphasis.

There are also changes proposed for radio. A new Radio Authority is to run commercial radio instead of the IBA. It is to administer the introduction of three new national radio stations, as well as many new community radio stations.

**Source 3.15**
The table shows how broadcasting is to be regulated in Britain in the 1990s. Which television service seems likely to provide the viewer with the most choice of programmes?

---

**WHAT INDEPENDENT TV & RADIO SERVICES MUST PROVIDE**

This table shows only the proposed programming requirements. Some services may well provide kinds of programmes they are not strictly *required* to – to cover minority interests for example.

| | TELEVISION | | | | | | RADIO | |
| --- | --- | --- | --- | --- | --- | --- | --- | --- |
| | Ch.3 | Ch.4 | Chs. 5&6 | Future DBS* | Other Satellite | Local TV | National | Local |
| Consumer protection (taste, decency, violence etc.) | ✓ | ✓ | ✓ | ✓ | ✓ | ✓ | ✓ | ✓ |
| High quality news and current affairs | ✓ | ✓ | ✓ | ✓ | ✗ | ✗ | ✗ | ✗ |
| Diverse programming | ✓ | ✓ | ✓ | ✗ | ✗ | ✗ | ✓ | ✗ |
| Add to diversify of listener choice (new stations) | — | — | — | — | — | — | — | ✓ |
| Regional programmes | ✓ | ✗ | ✗ | ✗ | ✗ | ✗ | ✗ | ✗ |
| Educational programmes** | ✗ | ✓ | ✗ | ✗ | ✗ | ✗ | ✗ | ✗ |
| At least 25% of programmes from independent producers | ✓ | ✓ | ✓ | ✓ | ✗ | ✗ | — | — |
| Proper proportion of programmes to be produced in UK or other European Community country | ✓ | ✓ | ✓ | ✓ | ✗ | ✗ | — | — |

BBC1, BBC2, and BBC radio will continue to be subject to the full range of public service obligations. Channel 4 will continue to have a remit to provide innovative and minority interest programmes
*For any further channels allocated under new legislation.*
** In addition, the ITC will have a duty to arrange for schools programmes by independent TV

**Source 3.15** (*Independent,* 9 Nov. 1988)

Compare the programmes listed in the American television schedules with the choice offered by British television for a similar time. What is the effect of having entertainment as the main aim of television?

*Source 3.16*  American Television (*American TV Guide*, Triangle, July 1987)

## Other regulatory bodies

### 1. *The Press Council*

This passes judgement on complaints made about stories appearing in the press. It considers about 60 cases a year. However, it has no power to force newspapers to maintain standards or print apologies for inaccurate journalism. Many of its rulings are ignored. This has led many people to call for stricter controls, possibly including laws which would protect an individual's right to privacy (e.g., members of the Royal Family) or provide a right of reply to those who have been (often unfairly) attacked by the press. However, these controls might restrict further the freedom of the press, especially its ability to uncover fraud and scandal amongst the more powerful sections of society.

### 2. *Advertising Standards Authority*

This also considers complaints made by the public, but unlike the Press Council, its rulings are taken note of by advertisers.

---

### Friday
**6 PM – 7:30 PM**

Program chart is on A-124
Pay-TV movie details begin on A-8

July 24, 1987

### Friday
**7:30 PM – 8 PM**

**(51)** SECRET CITY—Children
Tips on creating origami birds.
**(57)** WE'RE COOKING NOW
**(63)** GOMER PYLE, USMC
Gomer's pet crow likes stealing from everyone—and stashing the loot in Gomer's locker.
**(A&E)** SKAG—Drama; 60 min.
**(BET)** SOFT NOTES—Music; 60 min.
**(CBN)** BIG VALLEY—Western; 60 min.
**(DIS)** MOUSETERPIECE THEATER—Cartoon
**(HTS)** WORLD IN HARNESS—Harness Racing
**(LIF)** LADY BLUE—Crime Drama; 60 min.
**(NSH)** CROOK AND CHASE—Magazine
**(SHO)** JUST FRIENDS—Teen-agers; 50 min.
**(USA)** CARTOON EXPRESS; 60 min.
**6:05 (TBS)** DOWN TO EARTH—Comedy
Lissy brings an exchange student home.
**6:30 (3) (6)** CBS NEWS—Dan Rather
**(3) (8) (13)** ABC NEWS—Peter Jennings
**(5W)** TOO CLOSE FOR COMFORT—Comedy
**(10) (12) (29)** NBC NEWS—Tom Brokaw
**(19) (23) (51)** NIGHTLY BUSINESS REPORT
Commentator: Charles Schultze.
**(20W)** PRIVATE BENJAMIN—Comedy
**(33)** CARTER COUNTRY—Comedy
On a diet, Chief Roy (Victor French) loses more friends than pounds.
**(57)** SECRET CITY—Children
Tips on creating origami birds.
**(63)** ANDY GRIFFITH—Comedy (BW)
Mayberry gets spooked when a newcomer seems to know all about them.
**(CNN)** SHOWBIZ TODAY—Wickersham/Leonard
**(DIS)** ZORRO—Adventure (BW)
**(HBO)** MOVIE (CC)—Drama; 2 hrs., 15 min.
"Death of a Salesman."
**(HTS)** WEIGHT TRAINING—Commercial
**(MAX)** MOVIE—Drama; 2 hrs., 25 min.
"Urban Cowboy."
**(NIK)** NICK ROCKS COUNTDOWN—Magazine
An interview with Jim Kerr (Simple Minds).
**(NSH)** VIDEOCOUNTRY
**6:35 (TBS)** LEAVE IT TO BEAVER (BW)
**7 PM (3)** NEWLYWED GAME
**(3) (8) (13)** WHEEL OF FORTUNE (CC)—Game
**(5W)** TAXI—Comedy
**(6)** NEWS
**(10)** ENTERTAINMENT TONIGHT—Magazine
Scheduled: Mark Harmon.
**(12)** M*A*S*H
Hawkeye falls for a Korean aristocrat (Kieu Chinh). Alan Alda, Harry Morgan.
**(19) (23) (51)** MacNEIL, LEHRER NEWSHOUR; 60 min.
**(20W)** JEFFERSONS (CC)—Comedy
**(27)** SHOGUN—Drama; 3 hrs.
Part 3. Anjin-san's assimilation of Japanese ways is evident in his relationship with Mariko (Yoko Shimada), his conduct as a samurai and his reunion with his crew. Anjin-san: Richard Chamberlain. Toranaga: Toshiro Mifune.

Rodrigues: John Rhys-Davies. Father Alvito: Damien Thomas. Kiku: Mika Kitagawa. [Concludes Sat. 7 P.M.]
**(29)** M*A*S*H
Hawkeye cuts red tape to help a GI marry his child's Korean mother. Hawkeye: Alan Alda.
**(33)** FAME—Drama; 60 min.
Lydia tells Danny and Leroy that they can't appear in the Alumni Day program unless they do a favor for an alumnus: coach a children's basketball team. Carlo Imperato.
**(35)** GOOD TIMES
At her new job as a store detective, Willona (Ja'net DuBois) feels guilty about spying on the customers. J.J.: Jimmie Walker.
**(57)** BODY ELECTRIC—Exercise
**(63)** BUCK ROGERS—Science Fiction; 60 min.
Seven dwarf-like aliens, bent on making mischief, may wear out their welcome aboard the Searcher. Gil Gerard. Xces: Tommy Madden.
**(A&E)** ROCKLINE FROM LONDON—Music
**(BET)** VIDEO LP—Music
**(CBN)** HARDCASTLE AND McCORMICK—Crime Drama; 60 min.
**(CNN)** MONEYLINE—Lou Dobbs
**(DIS)** MOVIE—Adventure; 1 hr., 35 min.
"Way Down Cellar."
**(ESN)** SPORTSCENTER
**(HTS)** PENNANT CHASE—Baseball; 60 min.
**(LIF)** PEOPLE IN CRISIS—Discussion
Two sisters vie for the same men.
**(NIK)** YOU CAN'T DO THAT ON TELEVISION—Children
**(NSH)** YOU CAN BE A STAR—Talent Contest
**(SHO)** TALL TALES & LEGENDS (CC)—Fantasy; 60 min.
"Ponce De Leon and the Search for the Fountain of Youth." Michael York plays the age-conscious Spanish explorer who discovers Florida. Sally Kellerman, Paul Rodriguez.
**(TMC)** MOVIE (CC)—Comedy; 1 hr., 40 min.
"Gotcha!"
**(USA)** AIRWOLF—Adventure; 60 min.
**7:05 (TBS)** SANFORD AND SON—Comedy
**7:30 (3)** DATING GAME
**(3) (8) (13)** JEOPARDY! (CC)—Game
**(5W)** M*A*S*H
**(6)** NEWLYWED GAME
**(10)** HOLLYWOOD SQUARES—Game
Ahmad Rashad, Arleen Sorkin, Jose Feliciano, Betty White, Brad Garrett, Pat McCormick.
**(12)** ENTERTAINMENT TONIGHT—Magazine
Scheduled: Mark Harmon, who discusses his movie "Summer School."
**(20W)** BENSON—Comedy
**(29)** M*A*S*H
Everyone wants to mother a wounded and apparently orphaned Korean boy (Edgar Raymond Miller). Alan Alda, Wayne Rogers.
**(35)** SANFORD AND SON—Comedy
After he comes home from a trip, Fred (Redd

Foxx) gets the mistaken idea that Lamont doesn't want him back.
**(57)** NIGHTLY BUSINESS REPORT
Commentator: Charles Schultze.
**(A&E)** RISING DAMP—Comedy
Rigsby tries to spook Alan by telling him the boardinghouse is haunted. Leonard Rossiter.
**(BET)** NEWS
**(CNN)** CROSSFIRE—Braden/Novak
**(ESN)** U.S. OLYMPIC FESTIVAL; 3 hrs., 30 min.
Included: track and field, women's gymnastics (team all-around competition) and taekwondo finals. Telecast from sites in central North Carolina. (Live)
**(LIF)** OUR GROUP—Drama
A phony psychic dupes a woman in search of her identity.
**(NIK)** SPARTAKUS—Cartoon
**(NSH)** FANDANGO—Game
**7:35 (TBS)** BASEBALL
Atlanta at Philadelphia. (Live)
**8 PM (3) (6)** BUGS BUNNY/LOONEY TUNES JUBILEE (CC)—Cartoon; 60 min.
From 1986: Hollywood toasts Bugs, Porky Pig, Daffy Duck and friends with clips and quips on their golden jubilee. The testimonial features David Bowie, Cher, Candice Bergen, Steve Martin, Chevy Chase, Bill Murray, Penny Marshall and Chuck Yeager; and clips from cartoon classics like "Ali Baba Bunny" (1956) and "Knighty Knight Bugs" (1958). (Repeat)
**(3) (13)** SLEDGE HAMMER! (CC)—Comedy
Hammer (David Rasche) has a run-in with a defecting Soviet scientist, and winds up protecting him from the KGB. Professor: Mark Blankfield. (Repeat)
**(5W)** SPRING BREAK REUNION—Variety; 2 hrs.
The party atmosphere of Fort Lauderdale, Fla., provides the backdrop for a beach bash reminiscent of the 1950s and '60s, with performances by Jan and Dean, the Ventures, the Drifters, the Crystals, Del Shannon.
**(8)** OUR PRIVATE HOPE: LEARN TO READ
A documentary chronicling the success of the Learn to Read program in Virginia.
**(10) (12) (29)** STINGRAY—Crime Drama; 60 min.
A military-school cadet is the victim of hazing and a series of "accidents" after he witnesses a murder committed by upperclassmen. Stingray: Nick Mancuso. (Repeat)
Guest Cast
Tom O'Connor . . . . . . . . . . . . . . . Doug Savant
Sgt. Jeff Callahan . . . . . . . . . George McDaniel
Anthony Santini . . . . . . . . . . . . . . Bill Calvert
Frederickson . . . . . . . . . James A. Watson Jr.
Commandant Hart . . . . . . . . . . . Joe Higgins
**(19) (23) (51)** WASHINGTON WEEK IN REVIEW (CC)
**(20W)** MOVIE—Thriller; 2 hrs., 30 min.
"The Fury." (1978) Kirk Douglas as a father

## Appendix H
## Advertising of cigarettes

*Introduction*

1.9  The essence of the Code is that advertisements should not seek to encourage people, particularly the young, to start smoking or, if they are already smokers, to increase their level of smoking, or to smoke to excess; and should not exploit those who are especially vulnerable, in particular young people and those who suffer from any physical, mental or social handicap.

*Rules*

2.1  Advertisements should not seek to persuade people to start smoking.

2.2  Advertisements should not seek to encourage smokers to smoke more or smoke to excess; or show a cigarette left in the mouth.

2.3  Advertisements should not exaggerate the attractions of smoking.

2.4  Advertisements should not exploit those who are especially vulnerable, whether on account of their youth or immaturity or as a result of any physical, mental or social handicap.

2.5  Advertisements should not claim directly or indirectly that it is natural to smoke, or that it is abnormal not to smoke.

2.6  Advertisements should not claim or imply that smoking is healthy or free from risk to health.

2.7  Advertisements should not claim directly or indirectly that smoking is a necessity for relaxation or for concentration.

2.8  Advertisements should not claim directly or indirectly that to smoke, or to smoke a particular brand

(a) is a sign or proof of manliness, courage or daring.

(b) enhances feminine charm.

2.9  Advertisements should not include or imply any personal testimonial for, or recommendation of a particular brand by any group or class of people engaged in an activity or calling which particularly attracts public admiration or emulation.

2.10  Advertisements should not include copy or illustrations which are sexually titillating or which imply a link between smoking and sexual success; nor should any advertisement contain any demonstration of affection in such a way as to suggest romantic or sexual involvement between those portrayed.

2.11  Advertisements should not claim directly or indirectly that it contributes significantly to the attainment of social or business success to smoke, or to smoke a particular brand.

2.12  No advertisements should appear in any publication directed wholly or mainly to young people.

2.13  Advertisements should not feature heroes of the young.

2.14  Advertisements should not imply that smoking is associated with success in sport. They should not depict people participating in any active sporting pursuit or obviously about to do so or just having done so, or spectators at any organised sporting occasion. NB: Advertising associated with events sponsored by cigarette manufacturers is subject to separate rules.

***Source 3.17***  Advertising code for cigarettes

***Source 3.17***  (*Advertising Standards Authority*)

**Source 3.18**

How do these two cigarette adverts offend against the code described in source 3.17? (NB: these adverts pre-date the present code.)

**3.** *Broadcasting Complaints Commission*

This was established in 1980 and deals with complaints made against the BBC and ITV. It can force either organisation to broadcast apologies. However, this rarely happens. In 1985, only 10 complaints were supported from 218 made to the Commission.

**4.** *Broadcasting Standards Council*

Set up in 1988, its brief is to reinforce standards of decency and taste, particularly with regard to the portrayal of sex and violence, and bad language.

# GOLD LEAF
## are made for the smoker who knows what he wants...

taste!

GOLD LEAF TASTE GOOD!

You get more to enjoy with Kensitas Corsair

**Source 3.18**

One reason why external controls from the government and regulatory bodies may not often be used is that those working within the media regulate themselves.

# Media professionals

In any large organisation, there is a division of labour with special tasks performed by those with the skill and training. This means that the **owners** (usually the shareholders) are often not the **controllers** (those who decide what is made) or the **media professionals** (those who are employed to make television programmes, write newspapers etc.).

## Activity

From any one of the main media, try and identify:
1. The different roles of those involved in producing a television programme, magazine, record, etc. The key contributors are often mentioned in credit lists, e.g. at the front of a magazine, or at the end of a film or television programme.
2. The different stages through which a product is assembled. A flow chart may be helpful here.

## News production

Every individual joining an organisation soon learns what is expected of him/her in terms of good practice and standards. This can be seen with the example of news production.

### 1. *Sources*

News does not simply flow into newsrooms. Much of it can be predicted and planned for in advance. Furthermore, some organisations can be relied on to supply a constant stream of stories, e.g. the police and courts.

*Source 3.19*   News sources
From a television or radio news bulletin, or a national daily newspaper, try and identify as many of the sources of news from the checklist below.

### Sources monitored routinely

1. Parliament
2. Councils
3. Police (and the army in Northern Ireland)
4. Other emergency services
5. Courts (including inquests and tribunals)
6. Royalty
7. 'Diary' events (e.g. annual events like Ascot or conferences known about in advance)
8. Airports
9. Other news media

### Organisations issuing statements and holding press conferences

10. Government departments
11. Local authority departments
12. Public services (transport authorities, electricity boards, etc.)
13. Companies
14. Trade unions
15. Non-commercial organisations (pressure groups, charities, etc.)
16. Political parties
17. Army, Navy, Air Force

### Individuals making statements, seeking publicity, etc.

18. Prominent people (e.g. Bishops and film stars)
19. Members of the public

*Source 3.19*   (B. Whitaker, *News United*, Minority Press Group, 1981)

### 2. *Processing and selection*

Each day, those who produce the news have to decide which news should be covered, and how it should be presented. These decisions are often referred to as **gatekeeping**. There are several people who act as gatekeepers in processing the news on television, radio or in the press, from the journalist up to the senior editor.

## The production cycle

| News Sources | Selection | Gathering/Processing |
|---|---|---|
| A. Predicted news Diary events, Parliament Royalty, reports, trials, etc. | 1. The evening before | Camera/Sound crews Reporters |
| B. News developments from predicted news and unexpected events | 2. Editorial conference | Delivery and processing |
| | 3. Rough running order | |
| | 4. Planned running order | |
| | | Editing, script writing and graphics |
| C. Late news | 5. Rehearsal and final selection | |
| | 6. News broadcast | |

### Activities

1. From an evening's television or radio news, try to decide when each story has been selected during the day. One clue could be gained from recording and viewing news broadcasts throughout the day.

2. From a 12-hour cycle of news (i.e. breakfast time to mid-evening), compile a chart showing how the running order of stories has changed.

### News values

Deciding what to include in the news, and which stories should be given most attention depends on judging their **newsworthiness**.

Some of the most important news values are:

1. *Drama/unexpectedness* – sudden, spectacular events.

2. *Personalities* – presenting news in relation to key individuals: the eye witness, the human survivor, famous celebrities, etc.

3. *Relevance* – its importance for national and local interest. Events happening far away have to be very dramatic to be covered.

4. *Immediacy* – things that have happened very recently, or

5. *Continuity* – events which are part of a 'running story'.

6. *Negativity* – bad news, disasters, threats, etc.

### Activity

Compare a popular tabloid newspaper like the *Sun* with a serious broadsheet newspaper like the *Independent* in terms of their news values. How have the editors decided what are the important stories?

### How they bring the news

**9.00 am** ● The producer of the day **1** arrives in the newsroom. Already, between a third and a half of the programme has been "blocked off" to make room for expected material. Today, for instance, Trevor McDonald will be sending a report on South Africa. There is also the TUC conference in Blackpool, an event which *Channel Four News* is bound to cover. There are several options for news material. Peter Sissons, the programme presenter, may interview trade union leaders, or reporters may send packaged (edited) material down the line to London.

**10.30 am** ● Both *Channel Four News* **2** and Channel One (*News at One*, the *5.45 News* and *News at Ten*) hold editorial conferences to decide which "on-the-day" stories they will cover. *Channel Four News* sends an observer to the Channel One conference, to check what the Channel One programmes are doing. *Channel Four News* relies heavily on the *5.45 News* for the "hard news" for its summary. At the same time, *Channel Four News* will send its own crews on its own on-the-day stories.

**2.30 pm** ● Editor's conference, **3** attended by the presenters, the home and foreign editors and senior editorial staff. There is a rough running order of items, but the top story is only provisional. Often a story's chances will depend on whether the programme can get an interview. When Dr Allan Boesak was arrested in Cape Town, *Channel Four News* needed to get a reaction from Desmond Tutu. This in turn depended on whether they could get a satellite link. In the event, link and interview went ahead.

**4.30 pm** ● A running order is circulated. **4** The reporters are returning with their film. Now the process of assembly is underway, as people in charge of captions, slides, graphics, computer graphics, videotape editing and sound dubbing get to work on the "packages," as the finished news items are called. There are almost 2,000 different sound effects, from oars splashing to cars crashing. The most sought-after effect, curiously, is the sound of silence inside a house.

**7.00 pm** ● The programme goes on the **6** air. The producer will not have seen how the whole thing looks until this moment. Only the top story is likely to have been rehearsed.

Right up to transmission, *Channel Four News* can deal comprehensively with late-breaking news (this is what really distinguishes it from *Newsnight*). The news of the football disaster at the Heysel Stadium broke five minutes before the producer of the day went down to the control room.

*Source 3.20*   Channel 4 News (*New Society*, 4 Oct. 1985)

**Visuals** create another news value. Newspapers may run a story, if they have an appropriate photograph to use. Television relies very heavily on visual images to go with their stories, whereas for radio this obviously does not matter.

---

### Activity

Compare a radio and television news broadcast (preferably at roughly the same time of day). List the running order of stories on each. How far has the availability of pictures influenced the television selection?

---

### Pop music gatekeepers

Of the 6000 or so singles (3000) and albums (3000) released each year in Britain, only about 7–8% become chart hits (i.e. reach the top 30). That does not include all those musicians and performers making DIY records and tapes, or who never obtain any kind of record contract. As with the production of news there are various **gatekeepers** filtering the music before it reaches the public.

*Source 3.21*

*Source 3.22*

1. From the airplay list (source 3.22a), what is the relationship between radio plays and the chart position of a record?

2. How much do the BBC and ILR record playlists differ? (Consult the list, but also the selections of individual disc jockeys on the radio.) Why is this?

3. Apart from radio airplay, how else can a record become popular?

---

### Deciding what reaches the public

Record producers know that their clients' music won't reach its audience directly but will be mediated through a further set of gatekeepers – disc jockeys, concert promoters and so forth. A 'commercial' sound is not just a matter of public approval – to be commercial it first has to reach that public; hence, the studio emphasis on the single, a track aimed explicitly at radio station playlists. Decisions about how a record should sound can't be separated from a further set of decisions about how that sound will reach its most likely listeners, how it will be promoted and sold . . .

### Radio

Most record companies agree, however, that the most effective form of promotion is airplay. Telling people to listen to a record isn't the same as making them hear it, and one spin on the radio is worth any number of full-page ads or good reviews in the music press. To sell a record, companies must, in the end, get a *sound* to the public and to do this they have to go through a disc jockey, the most significant rock 'gatekeeper' . . .

*Source 3.21* (S. Frith, *Sound Effects*, Constable, 1983)

*Source 3.22a Music Week*, 24 Oct. 1987)

## Putting it together

*How a music playlist works*
In ILR, for example, the 'A' list is predominantly made up of current 'hit' singles. The 'B' list is usually new releases and chart 'climbers'. Some stations operate a 'C' list which might contain selected albums or releases at the more extreme ends of the musical spectrum. The 'oldies' are listed separately and are often referred to as 'golden oldies' or 'gold' for short. This list might be further subdivided (*see diagram*). Each list has a predetermined 'priority' which means each disc will be guaranteed a minimum number of 'plays' over the course of a day or week. 'A' listed records invariably have more frequent plays that those on the 'B' or 'C' lists.

The order in which records from each list appear in the output is then drawn up. The diagram illustrates the running order in a typical clock hour.

*This diagram shows the order in which records from each list might appear in a typical clock-hour.*

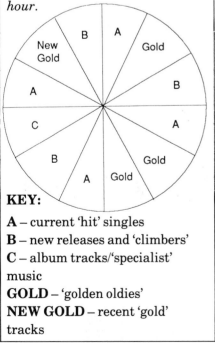

**KEY:**

**A** – current 'hit' singles
**B** – new releases and 'climbers'
**C** – album tracks/'specialist' music
**GOLD** – 'golden oldies'
**NEW GOLD** – recent 'gold' tracks

*Source 3.22b* (*Television and Radio*, 1988)

## How much freedom?

Media professionals rarely have the freedom to do as they please. Apart from having to work as part of a team, they have to consider the needs of their employers, the law, and not least, the audience. Which influence is greatest varies according to the situation.

*Source 3.23*
In each of the four examples (to the right and on page 54), what influences on media production seem to be at work?

# BBC claims Christmas ratings victory

By Dennis Barker

THE BBC maintained yesterday that ITV's claim to victory over the Christmas period was based on "cooked" figures and that the BBC had the highest rating over the whole Christmas week.

Mr Michael Grade, controller of BBC-1, said that ITV had "invented the three-day week" by announcing their proposed victory for the three days of Christmas Eve, Christmas Day, and Boxing Day alone.

Figures for the whole week, issued yesterday by the Broadcaster Audience Research Board, showed that the BBC repeat of Porridge had been watched by more people than anything else during the week December 20-26.

Porridge, screened the day after Boxing Day, had a rating of 19.36 million, whereas ITV's Christmas Day film Raiders of the Lost Ark had 19.33 million, said Mr Grade.

He also complained that even for the three days they covered, the figures issued by the ITV companies were inaccurate. They had claimed 18.5 million for the film Airplane! whereas the BARB figure was 18.1 million, and had said that the BBC's Escape To Victory had 14.9 million viewers, whereas it actually had 15.2 million.

The BARB figures gave the BBC audience share for the week as 50.4 per cent, compared to ITV's 49.6 per cent. The five BBC programmes in the top ten were Porridge, Kramer Versus Kramer, Mary Poppins, The Kenny Everett Show, and the Christmas edition of Blankety Blank.

Mr Grade said : "The reason they invented the three day week was that they knew they hadn't won Christmas Day itself, and they had to compile a three-day chart in order to hide the fact."

BBC researchers said that 92.6 million people had switched BBC during Christmas week, compared with 92.1 million watching ITV.

The success of the Christmas repeat of the Porridge episode coincided with talks about a possible new series. "We have discussed a new series with Ronnie Barker," said Mr Grave.

*Source 3.23a* (*The Guardian*, Jan. 1986)

# Court bans BBC security interview

ine Government last night obtained an injunction preventing the BBC from broadcasting any programme containing interviews with past or present members of the security and intelligence services, or including information obtained from them.

The injunction was granted on the eve of this morning's broadcast of the first of three programmes in a Radio 4 series, My Country Right or Wrong, featuring interviews with three former members of MI5, three former MI6 agents, and two ex-GCHQ employees. A serving GCHQ official also agreed to speak.

Mr John Birt, the BBC's deputy director-general responsible for news and current affairs, described the injunction as draconian. It had stopped the BBC from broadcasting all information of whatever kind about the security services from former members.

The process of making the programmes was open and the project was widely known within Government, including the security services, Mr Birt said.

The series is understood to include no new revelations. The intention was to give a general picture of the views and attitudes of those with experience of the security and intelligence agencies.

Ms Cathy Massiter, the former MI5 officer, who described on television two years ago how the security service tapped the telephones of Campaign for Nuclear Disarmament activists and leftwing trade unionists was to have taken part.

All but one of the former British officials, who were to have appeared, agreed to be named.

Six former CIA agents and two KGB defectors were also interviewed for the programmes, produced by Anne Sloman and Sheila Cook.

Labour MPs last night demanded an early Commons explanantion from the Attorney General, Sir Patrick Mayhew.

The shadow Attorney General, Mr John Morris, said that the move demonstrated that "Britain was rapidly becoming a police state."

The injunction was granted by Mr Justice Henry in a half-hour private hearing. A BBC lawyer said that an appeal was being considered.

The government decision to seek an injunction coincides with a High Court trial in which it is seeking permanent injunctions preventing the Guardian and Observer from commenting on allegations in Spycatcher, the memoirs of the former MI5 officer, Mr Peter Wright.

*Source 3.23b* (*The Guardian* Dec. 1987)

*Source 3.23c* (*The Sun*, 15 May 1984)

*Source 3.23d* (*Daily Mirror*, 9 June 1983)

# Case study: EastEnders

This chapter has been about the media as an **institution**. Having considered the influences on media production such as ownership, the need for profit, the law, professional practice, etc., it is necessary to bring in the audience (discussed at length in chapter 6). To answer the question posed at the beginning of the chapter — 'What brings producers and audiences together, and how is the relationship between them shaped?' — let us consider the case of a successful media product, the BBC's *EastEnders*.

**Figure 3.7**

### EastEnders: The Research Contribution

On February 19th 1985 the BBC launched its new twice-weekly serial *EastEnders*. It was the BBC's first major soap opera since the 1960s . . . The idea of producing a twice-weekly, year-round serial had originated in June 1981, and was promoted by an acute problem. BBC-1's early evening weekday audience performance was poor. Instead of winning viewers in the early part of the evening who might stay with the channel for the rest of the night, BBC-1's early evening audience fell off between 6.30 and 7.30 p.m. . . . Practical production considerations such as budgets, production teams, studios and so on determined that decisions on the fundamental basis for the serial, like where it would be located, were taken very early on in the planning stages . . . Julia Smith had a clear idea of what she wanted to do but felt that her ideas would benefit from research and the views of the potential audience . . . London emerged as an acceptable location, which coincided with the location Julia

Smith had in mind: 'I knew all along what I really wanted to do, which was a series set in the East End of London. I'm a Londoner. All other soaps come from a different part of the country and I felt that the South was entitled to its own. I think the Cockneys have a vitality and a basic humour which is a necessary ingredient for a soap.' (Julia Smith, *The Times*, 1985).

In view of the 'dated' impressions of many other British soaps, potential viewers wanted the serial to address itself to current issues and concerns . . .

### February 1985: EastEnders goes on air

After a year of intense activity, amidst a blaze of publicity and considerable press and public sceptism, *EastEnders* went on air on February 19th 1985 at 7.00 p.m. It was dubbed by the press as 'the BBC's belated challenge to *Coronation Street*, (Bhegani, *Time Out*, 1985) and by the public as 'Just another *Coronation Street* in the South' (*Group Discussions*, 1985). The BBC, however hoped that by regularly scheduling it on

*Source 3.24* (*BBC Research Findings*, BBC)

Tuesdays and Thursdays at 7.00 p.m. it would reverse the early evening dip in audience ratings . . .

*EastEnders* started fairly strongly, the audience dipped during the spring and summer and from the autumn it started to build a loyal audience of its own, reaching an all time high of 23 million over Christmas, less than a year after it was first shown . . .

In common with other soaps *EastEnders* was initially most popular amongst women, older people and those in the working-class groups, but unusually for soaps it was not outstandingly more popular in the North than in the South. Unlike other soaps, after the first few tentative months the appeal of the serial extended across age groups and social class groups and a year after it was launched *EastEnders* had the widest appeal of any soap opera on British television . . .

By August it was improving on its share of viewers and was beginning to establish a following. Further steps were needed to consolidate and improve its position in the autumn, and these were taken when, as part of the new autumn schedules, *EastEnders* was re-scheduled from 7.00 p.m. to 7.30 p.m. on Tuesdays and Thursdays.

*Autumn 1985*
The move to 7.30 p.m. coincided with extensive media coverage of *EastEnders* story-lines, particularly in the 'who dunnit?' scandal surrounding school-girl Michelle Fowler's pregnancy. *EastEnders'* stories and its actors started to receive intense media interest . . .

Increasingly numbers of viewers were making a conscious decision to make *EastEnders* a part of their regular weekly routine. . . . Viewers revealed that they now structured their lives around the programme, and that *EastEnders* had become a part of their social interaction. Viewers spoke about the characters as if they knew them well and elements of fact and fiction about the characters and actors had inevitably become blurred. The strengths of the serial were seen to lie in its confrontation of contemporary moral and social issues and its responsible treatment of 'delicate' subjects – the cot death and teenage pregnancy came in for special mention.

***Source 3.24***   The development of EastEnders
From the description of *EastEnders* development, draw a flow chart showing how each of the following influenced its rise to popularity:
1. the ratings
2. the location
3. the themes of the serial
4. press reaction
5. scheduling
6. audience response.

***Source 3.24***   (Continued from page 55)

# ▌New technology

Much has been said about the 'technological revolution' in recent years. The use of small and cheap computer chips to store and relay huge amounts of information means the television is no longer just a means of showing pictures beamed by traditional transmitters. It can now be linked to several other sources of information and entertainment.

***Source 3.25***  Television and new technology

**Activity**

Choose one of the new technologies which can be used with television, and describe its possible uses.

### Consequences

The effects of new technology cannot be easily assessed. Much depends on how the technology relates to the existing media institution.

**1.** *Cable and satellite*

***Source 3.26***

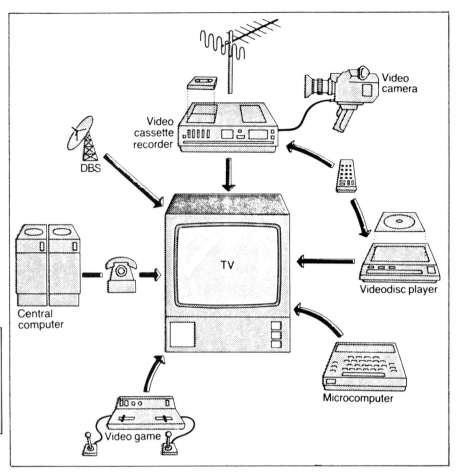

***Source 3.25***  The Video Revolution. A modern television can display information from a variety of sources. (J. Megarry, *Inside Information*, BBC, 1985)

---

**Cable will do more than change television. It will change our lives.**

This technological revolution will have fundamental and far-reaching effects on what we are offered in conventional television news and entertainment, but will do much more than simply change the nature of our evenings at home. For its aim is to change the whole mechanics of our society.

Multi-channel cable will act as a common carrier system. It will be owned and operated either by the Post Office or by private investors. But those who own the cables are unlikely to originate what they carry; they will simply rent out space.

Though it will have the effect of enormously increasing 'broadcasting' – transmitting to millions of people over continents – it will also introduce the equally important facility of 'narrowcasting' – sending messages to carefully selected specialist audiences. And it is this facility which industry and commerce most eagerly await.

The BBC and big ITV companies will still be in the business of broadcasting as we know it, but they will concentrate most on events like the Coronation of Charles III, which will bring the whole nation together in front of their TV sets. But it is unlikely that BBC and ITV will provide large-scale entertainment programmes in the 1990s.

Instead, these will become the province of large international and multi-national broadcasters, beaming not just to nations, but to entire continents by TV satellites.

***Source 3.26***  (*Sunday Times*, 7 Dec. 1980)

## sunday

### SUPER CHANNEL
07 00 The Smooch
08 00 Funbus
08 05 Henry's Cat
08 10 Beany and Cecil
08 20 Heathcliff
08 30 Take Hart
09 00 TBA
10 00 Macron I
10 30 The Norway Cup
11 00 TBA
11 30 Videopix
12 30 Lunch with a Star
13 30 Tomorrow's World at Large An Explosive Situation
14 00 Frontline
15 00 TBA
15 10 The Goodyear Weather Forecast
15 15 What the European Papers Say
15 30 Super Sport with Paul McDowell
17 00 The European Hot 100
18 00 The Muppet Show Command Performance
18 30 Rafferty's Rules
19 25 The Goodyear Weather Forecast
19 30 Benny Hill
20 30 Some Mothers Do 'Ave 'Em comedy series
21 00 Love and Marriage Dearly Beloved
22 00 Tales of the Unexpected
22 30 The Goodyear Weather Forecast
22 35 Feature Film
01 00 Simon Potter
02 00 Amanda Redington
03 00 The Buzz Tony Dortie with concert news, tour dates and hot gossip
04 00 Music Box Live with Nino Firetto
05 00 Countdown with Adam Curry
06 00 The Face

### THE CHILDREN'S CHANNEL
05 00 Cartoon Time including Cool McCool, Johnny the Pea, Shazam, Leo and Fred, Popeye, Koketo and Murr
06 00 Saturdee
06 30 Black Beauty
07 00 Cartoon Time including Cool McCool, Johnny the Pea, Shazam, Leo and Fred, Koketo and Murr
08 00 You Can't Do That on Television
08 30 Flash Forward
09 00 Saturdee

---

09 30 Black Beauty
10 00 Steve Moorewood Presents......
11 00 Cartoon Time including Cool McCool, Johnny the Pea, Shazam, Leo and Fred, Popeye, Koketo and Murr
12 00 You Can't Do That on Television
12 30 Flash Forward
13 30 Black Beauty
14 00 Steve Moorewood Presents......
15 00 Closedown

### SKY CHANNEL
08 00 Fun Factory Sky's children's programmes with Andy, Snoot and Crocker
08 00 Emily
08 05 Popeye
08 10 The Poppies
08 25 Dennis
08 40 Return to the Planet of the Apes
09 15 Inspector Gadget
09 45 He-Man
10 15 Mask
10 35 Jayce & the Wheeled Warriors
11 10 Bailey's Bird
11 40 Transformers
12 05 The American Show the US pop chart sounds
12 35 Young, Free and Single music and favourite videos from the charts
13 05 UK Despatch music and guest interviews from London
13 35 Heartline Tony Blackburn with viewers musical dedications
14 35 US College Football 1987 top American College football games
15 35 VFL Australian Rules Football
16 35 Flying Kiwi adventure series
17 05 Swatch Fashion TV fashion and news reports
17 30 The Coca-Cola Eurochart Top 50 Show
18 30 Daniel Boone western series
19 25 Fantasy Island adventure series
20 20 Beulah Land — Mini Series part 1 starring Lesley Ann Warren, Hope Lange, Michael Sarrazin and Meredith Baxter Birney
22 05 VFL Australian Football
23 05 The Coca-Cola Eurochart Top 50 Show
00 05 Heartline Tony Blackburn with viewers musical dedications
01 05 Closedown

### SSAT
18 00 Anderland. Unerhort
18 30 Weana Gmuat Wien und seine Musik in Anekdoten
19 00 Heute
19 10 3SAT - Studio

---

19 30 Wetten, daß...? Mit Thomas Gottschalk
21 15 Ein Haus voll Geschichten Das Historische Museum in Wien wird 100 Jahre alt
21 40 Lil Dagover zum 123. Geburtstag. Der müde Tod Deutscher Spielfilm
23 30 3SAT - Schlagzeilen

### FILMNET
MORNING CLUB
07 30 Pete's Dragon
09 15 Snoopy Come Home
11 00 How to Marry a Millionaire
12 45 The Mark
ROYAL CLUB
15 00 Bluebeards Eighth Wife
17 00 Wholly Moses
19 00 21 Hours at Munich
21 00 Three in the Cellar
NIGHT CLUB
23 00 30 is a Dangerous Age, Cynthia
01 00 National Lampoons Movie Madness
03 00 Thief of Hearts
05 00 The Naked Face

### SCREEN SPORT
17 00 Wide World of Sports (R)
18 00 Worldwide Wrestling (R)
19 00 Rallycross Day 1 of the European Champs from Lydden Hill
20 30 Speedway Match of the Week
21 30 Stox Racing
22 30 Auto Racing IMSA GTP from Texas (R)
24 00 Close

### LIFESTYLE
09 00 Jack's Game
09 30 Donahue
10 30 Farmhouse Kitchen
11 00 Search for Tomorrow Omnibus

### SAT 1
16 30 SAT 1-1hr privates programm
16 35 Tier + Wir
17 00 Ich suche einen Mann Filmlustspiel
18 30 SAT 1 blick Nachrichten Und Wetter
18 45 Bezaubernde Jeannie
19 15 SAT 1 blick Schlagzeilen
19 20 Hotel
20 10 SAT 1 blick Schlagzeilen
20 15 Angelique und der Sultan Spielfilm
22 05 Polizeirevier Hill Street
22 55 SAT 1 blick Berichte Vom Tage, Sport Und Wetter
23 10 Stunde der Filmemacher

### THE ARTS CHANNEL
06 00 Otello
08 30 Stephen Calloway
09 00 Close

---

### TV5
14 00 Apostrophes Les choses de la vie Magazine littéraire
15 15 L'École Des Fans Variétés
15 50 Aujourd'hui En France Reportage
16 00 Sports Magazine
18 00 Bonjour Bon Appetit Magazine culinaire
18 30 Le Mot Juste Jeu
19 00 A La Folie Pas Du Tout Divertissement
20 00 Crimes Passionels Antoinette Serie fiction
21 00 Nouveaux Mondes L'Australie Serie documentaire
22 00 Journal Télévisé
22 30 7 Sur 7 Magazine d'actualités

### MTV
01 00-02 00 New Visions
10 00-11 45 The US Top 20 Video Countdown
19 00-20 00 XPO
22 00-23 00 Metal

### PREMIERE
15 00 D.A.R.Y.L. (PG)
16 40 Robotech Eps 77, 78 & 79 (U)
17 50 Street Legal Eps 4
18 40 King David (PG)
20 25 The Movie Club
20 50 Failing In Love (PG)
22 30 Mean Streets (18)
00 20 Tattooed Dragon (18)
02 00 October Review 1987
02 20 Dancin' To The Hits No 7 (PG)
02 50 Close

---

### SUPER CHANNEL
07 00 Hippo children's programme
08 00 Amanda Redington
09 00 Sons and Daughters drama series
09 30 Swim
10 00 TBA
10 15 What the European Papers Say
10 30 Emmerdale Farm drama series
11 00 Take Six Cooks
11 30 Simon Potter
12 30 The Name of the Game
14 00 The Goodyear Weather Forecast
14 05 Sons and Daughters drama series
14 30 Hippo children's programme
15 30 Macron I
16 00 Music Box Live with Nino Firetto
17 00 Countdown with Adam Curry
18 00 Family Entertainment
18 30 Doctor Who
19 00 Game Show
19 25 The Goodyear Weather Forecast
19 30 Survival Eagle Come Home
20 30 Three of a Kind — Montreux Special
21 00 Action Drama
22 00 Super Channel News International and business news
22 15 Super Channel News European and sports news
22 30 Super Sport
23 30 The Goodyear Weather Forecast
23 35 Frontline current affairs documentary
00 30 Spitting Image
01 00 Simon Potter
02 00 Amanda Redington
03 00 The Buzz Tony Dortie with concert news, tour dates and hot gossip
04 00 Music Box Live with Nino Firetto
05 00 Countdown with Adam Curry
06 00 The Face

### THE CHILDREN'S CHANNEL
05 00 Roustabout including Towser, Children's Island
05 30 My Little Pony & Friends, Bob's Your Uncle, Madame Gusto's Circus
06 30 Voltron
07 00 Roustabout including Towser, Children's Island
07 30 My Little Pony & Friends, Bob's Your Uncle, Madame Gusto's Circus
08 30 Voltron
09 00 Jack in the Box including Sing a Song, Sally and Jake, Silly Fairy Stories, Little Ghost, Orm & Cheep, The Dodo Club
10 00 Storytime including Simon,

---

Mouse on Mars, Bel the Minder, Bunny with Chequered Ears, Piggledy & Frederick, The Flumps, Tell Me a Story
11 00 Jack in the Box
13 00 Roustabout
15 00 Closedown

### SKY CHANNEL
07 30 The D.J. Kat Wake-Up Club
07 35 The D.J. Kat Show Sky's family entertainment show
08 35 New Music music magazine show
09 35 The Nescafe UK Network Top 40 Show The UK pop chart sounds
10 35 Sky Trax from Germany
11 05 The Smash Great Video Race music and phone-in competitions
12 05 The Coca-Cola Eurochart Top 50
13 05 Another World drama series
14 00 The Outsiders drama series
15 00 Transformers animated series
15 30 Barrier Reef adventure series
16 00 First Run the music tipped to be in the charts
16 30 Young, Free and Single music and favourite videos from the charts
17 00 The D.J. Kat Show Sky's family entertainment show
18 00 The Monkees comedy series
18 30 Hogan's Heroes comedy series
18 57 The Uniroyal Weather Report
19 00 The New Dick Van Dyke Show comedy series
19 30 Planet of the Apes futuristic series
20 25 Beulah Land — Mini Series part 2 starring Lesley Ann Warren, Hope Lange, Michael Sarrazin and Meredith Baxter Birney
22 07 The Uniroyal Weather Report
22 10 Mobil Motorsports News
22 40 Dutch Football 1987
23 40 The Nescafe UK Top 40 Show the UK pop chart sounds
00 37 The Uniroyal Weather Report
00 40 Closedown

### 3SAT
17 25 Mini-ZiB Nachrichten für Kinder
17 35 Wickie und die starken Manner Zeichentrickserie 1 Der Wettlauf
18 00 Sport-zeit
19 00 Heute
19 22 3SAT - Studio
19 30 Jugendmagazin
21 00 Kultur-Zeit

SATELLITE TV EUROPE September 1987 September 1987 SATELLITE TV EUROPE

---

***Source 3.27*** *(Satellite TV Europe, Sept 1987)*

***Source 3.27*** Cable/satellite schedules

***Source 3.28*** Lifestyle channel

***Source 3.29*** Wiring up Britain

1. How far are the claims made in *The Sunday Times* magazine (page 57) supported by the choice offered in the cable and satellite television schedule?
2. Does the *Lifestyle* channel programme description fit the idea of 'narrow casting' (i.e. sending messages to carefully selected audiences)?
3. Who had access to cable television in Britain in 1986? (See page 60.)

By 1989 satellite television is due to be available via two Direct Broadcast Satellites (DBS) stations *Astra* and *BSB*. The latter plans to offer four services: a news and sports channel, an entertainment channel, a daytime family service and a film channel. The popularity of such channels and their effect on BBC and ITV remain to be seen.

There is also the possibility of another technology supplying broadcasting in the future. **Microwave** television (MVDS) may provide up to 30 channels of over the air television in local areas using local high frequency transmitters. This may prove to be more practical and cheaper than cable in meeting local television needs.

**It Figures.** Charlene Pricket will help you keep fit with a complete exercise cycle for every part of the body. She will talk about physical problems like muscle strain and lower back pain.

**Good Sex!** The effervescent candour and contagious good humour of Dr. Westheimer (America's most popular sex educator) will amuse and inform you in a completely disarming way. She will answer questions on everything to do with sex.

Grace Mulligan bases her ...mhouse kitchen and ...vice, recipes and cookery ...well known cookery writers ...ks. She caters for all sizes of ...e families to people living

**The Sally Jessy Raphael Show.** Sally Jessy Raphael – a gleeful dynamo with bleached-blonde hair, red-rimmed glasses and fashionably tailored outfits – hosts her own American Emmy Award-winning talk show. She concentrates on "love, romance, human relationships and the fun things in life" with a wide variety of talkative and provocative guests.

**Baby & Co.** An innovative series by Dr. Miriam Stoppard encouraging parents to follow their own instincts and concentrate on what they think is best for their child. Does one child enable you to carry on your own life, but two or more mean they control you? What happens if mothers want to return to work? This programme has the answers.

**It's a Vet's life.** Veterinary surgeon John Baxter, ably assisted by Marilyn Webb, advises on all sorts of problems that pet owners may have. He also encounters such exotic species as boa constrictors and crocodiles.

*Source 3.28*

AT LAST! TV ABOUT YOU AND YOUR LIFE

LIFESTYLE

**7 DAYS** A WEEK, FROM BREAKFAST TIME TO EARLY AFTERNOON.

Lifestyle is something excitingly new in TV. For the first time, you can watch a whole range of programmes about family life as it affects you – dealing with a host of personal issues, from your diet to your spending, your health to your emotional relationships, your leisure to your lifestyle.

Lifestyle is television that reaches out to you in person, that comes into your home and talks about your experiences.

You'll find it frank and fascinating. Some of the absorbing programmes you can see are featured overleaf.

Lifestyles daily presenter is famous disc-jockey, TV Show host and announcer David Hamilton.

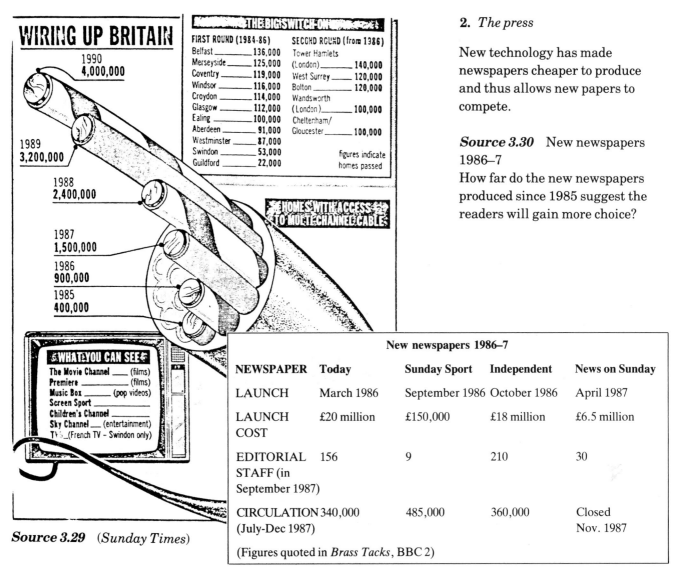

# WIRING UP BRITAIN

**1990** 4,000,000

**1989** 3,200,000

**1988** 2,400,000

**1987** 1,500,000

**1986** 900,000

**1985** 400,000

**THE BIG SWITCH-ON**

| FIRST ROUND (1984-86) | | SECOND ROUND (from 1986) | |
|---|---|---|---|
| Belfast | 136,000 | Tower Hamlets | |
| Merseyside | 125,000 | (London) | 140,000 |
| Coventry | 119,000 | West Surrey | 120,000 |
| Windsor | 116,000 | Bolton | 120,000 |
| Croydon | 114,000 | Wandsworth | |
| Glasgow | 112,000 | (London) | 100,000 |
| Ealing | 100,000 | Cheltenham/ | |
| Aberdeen | 91,000 | Gloucester | 100,000 |
| Westminster | 87,000 | | |
| Swindon | 53,000 | figures indicate | |
| Guildford | 22,000 | homes passed | |

**HOMES WITH ACCESS TO MULTI-CHANNEL CABLE**

**WHAT YOU CAN SEE**

The Movie Channel ___ (films)
Premiere ___ (films)
Music Box ___ (pop videos)
Screen Sport ___
Children's Channel ___
Sky Channel ___ (entertainment)
TV5 ___ (French TV – Swindon only)

**Source 3.29** (*Sunday Times*)

## 2. *The press*

New technology has made newspapers cheaper to produce and thus allows new papers to compete.

**Source 3.30** New newspapers 1986–7
How far do the new newspapers produced since 1985 suggest the readers will gain more choice?

| New newspapers 1986–7 | | | | |
|---|---|---|---|---|
| NEWSPAPER | Today | Sunday Sport | Independent | News on Sunday |
| LAUNCH | March 1986 | September 1986 | October 1986 | April 1987 |
| LAUNCH COST | £20 million | £150,000 | £18 million | £6.5 million |
| EDITORIAL STAFF (in September 1987) | 156 | 9 | 210 | 30 |
| CIRCULATION (July-Dec 1987) | 340,000 | 485,000 | 360,000 | Closed Nov. 1987 |

(Figures quoted in *Brass Tacks*, BBC 2)

**Source 3.30a**

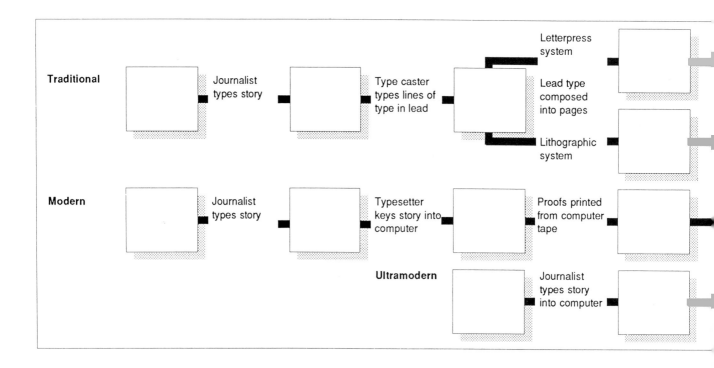

**Traditional** → Journalist types story → □ → Type caster types lines of type in lead → □ → Letterpress system / Lead type composed into pages / Lithographic system → □

**Modern** → Journalist types story → □ → Typesetter keys story into computer → □ → Proofs printed from computer tape → □

**Ultramodern** → Journalist types story into computer → □

## New technology: the key questions

### 1. Cost
What effect will the cost of new technology have for both producers and audiences? As an example, compare satellite television with pirate radio (see pages 40–1).

### 2. Audience needs
How will the new technology fit audience needs? Compare the Walkman and the videodisc for music audiences.

### 3. Regulation
How far will the government allow new technology to go unregulated? Consider the present controls on the BBC and ITV (see pages 44–6). How many of these controls will be possible with international satellite television stations?

**Source 3.30b**   (New newspapers, 1986–7)

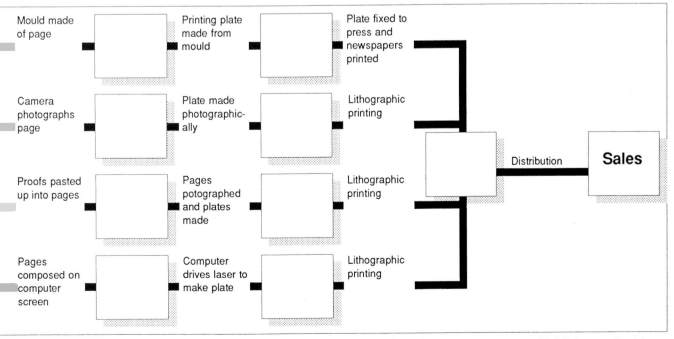

**Figure 3.8**   The impact of computer technology on the process of producing a newspaper  (J. Megarry, *Inside Information*, BBC, 1985)

INSTITUTIONS   61

# 4 REPRESENTATION

1. It is often said that television is a 'window on the world'. What do you think is meant by this statement?

2. How is looking at the world through a television screen different from looking at the world through a window in your house or classroom?

> **Activity**
>
> Select any television programme you regularly watch, and list everything you think you have learned from the programme.

It is not possible for the media to present the world as it really is (see pages 14 – 20). Because the media construct reality, they change or **mediate** what is really there. To mediate means to come between, and thereby to change or *re*present. Although much work goes into producing a natural 'this is the way the world is' picture of events, places, people, etc., it can never be pure or exact. This does not mean media professionals deliberately set out to misrepresent things, but simply that the printed word, the photograph, television picture, etc., all involve choices. It is always necessary to select and thus provide a particular way of seeing something. The news is a good example (see pages 50 – 52), but it applies equally to entertainment. The questions are what ideas, beliefs and attitudes are represented in the media?

*Figure 4.1* (*Airwaves*, IBA, Winter 1985/6)

# The world of advertising

## Source 4.1

What ideas are these adverts representing about each of the products?

**Source 4.1**

## Source 4.2

1. What is John Berger saying about the world of advertising? (NB: He refers to advertising as publicity.)
2. How far do you agree with his views?
3. Can his ideas be applied to the adverts above?

Publicity is always about the future buyer. It offers him an image of himself made glamorous by the product or opportunity it is trying to sell. The image then makes him envious of himself as he might be.

The spectator-buyer is meant to envy herself as she will become if she buys the product. She is meant to imagine herself transformed by the product into an object of envy for others, an envy which will then justify her loving herself.

The purpose of publicity is to make the spectator marginally dissatisfied with his present way of life. Not with the way of life of society, but with his own within it. It suggests that if he buys what it is offering, his life will become better. It offers him an improved alternative to what he is.

All publicity works upon anxiety. The sum of everything is money, to get money is to overcome anxiety.

Alternatively, the anxiety on which publicity plays is the fear that having nothing, you will be nothing.

**Source 4.2** (J. Berger, *Ways of Seeing,* Penguin, 1972)

# Stereotyping

## Source 4.3 Youth

1. What image of young people is represented here?
2. Who might have such ideas and why?

Stereotyping is labelling a whole group in a certain way, usually unfairly. For example, a stereotyped belief about people who live in the country is that they are old fashioned, suspicious of strangers and rather simple.

It is not easy to avoid using stereotypes. It enables us to generalise about people of whom we might not know very much. Teachers are as guilty of this as anyone – labelling pupils as stupid, hard-working, lazy, etc.

However, when one group stereotypes another it is often with the intention of controlling them. The result may be domination, exploitation and even violence. For example, Hitler promoted very strong anti-Jewish stereotyped ideas in the 1930s, which led eventually to Jews being murdered in concentration camps.

## Stereotyping and media representations

Representing groups in the media often involves stereotyping. There are even stereotypes of those working in the media such as football commentators, disc jockeys, tabloid journalists, etc.

## Source 4.4

1. Which stereotypes are represented in these pictures?
2. How might stereotypes help in achieving large audiences?
3. Which are the most common media stereotypes?

Brain that cannot read or do sums
Hair to dye pink and yellow
T shirt with suggestive message
Arm for holding onto boys in a crisis
Indecently tight jeans
shoes that "cost more than we earned in a week"
Head for butting opposition fans at football matches
Fat wallet full of money "we never had when we were young"
Felt tip pen for scrawling graffiti
knee for putting into old ladies
Boots for kicking in heads and telephone kiosks

**Source 4.3** (A. Bethell, *Viewpoint 2*, Thames TV, 1979)

a

b (L. Griffiths, *Arthur Daley's Guide to Doing it Right*, Willow, 1985)

c (*Radio Times*, 1 Nov. 1986)
**Source 4.4**

d (*Coronation Street, 25 years*, Granada, 1985)

# Gender representations

Males and females are often represented differently in the media.

## Source 4.5

1. How is masculinity and femininity signified in these adverts?
2. What do the terms masculine and feminine mean? Compare your answers with those of other members of your class.

Media representations of gender (i.e. masculinity and femininity) frequently use stereotyped ideas.

## Girls' and boys' worlds

**Source 4.6**   Girls' and boys' comics
How do the *Bunty* and *Victor* extracts (page 66) differ with respect to:

1. headings and layout
2. pictures and cartoons
3. topics of discussion
4. letters
5. any other differences

## Content analysis

This is a method of trying to discover whether there are any patterns or common features appearing in media content. After selecting suitable category headings, an attempt is made to count the number of examples appearing in the media, whether it be adverts, television fiction, newspaper stories, etc.

### Activity

Collect 4–6 weekly magazines, half of which are aimed at girls and half at boys. From the stories, make a list of:

1. The male and female roles, e.g. soldier, nurse, astronaut, mother, etc.
2. The settings of each story, e.g. the home, battle zone, hospital, etc.

From your results, make a table which shows the number and variety of roles and settings for each sex.

## Pop music and gender

In many respects, pop music has helped to break down some of the more traditional gender differences. It has long been accepted by audiences that male performers may wear make up, jewellery, and many different styles of clothes. Singers like David Bowie, Boy George, and even Michael Jackson, have challenged conventional ideas of what it is to look masculine. A few female performers, like Annie Lennox and Grace Jones, have rejected the dominant ideas of how to look feminine. However, there are still noticeable differences in the relationship between pop music and each gender.

*Source 4.5*

**Source 4.6a** (*Bunty*, 14 Nov. 1987)

**Source 4.6b** (*Victor*, 21 Nov. 1987)

**Source 4.7**

1. How does Simon Frith contrast the interests of boys and girls with rock music?
2. How does the profile of Ben from *My Guy* support this view?
3. Why do you think there are so few female musicians compared to singers?

**Activity**

With reference to **a.** appearance, and **b.** music, try to identify those singers and groups in the current top 30 who appeal to:

1. a mainly male audience
2. a mainly female audience
3. equally to both.

The teeny-bop idol's appeal is based on self-pity, vulnerability, and need. The image is the ideal boy next door: sad, thoughtful, pretty. Teeny-bop songs are about being let down and stood up, about loneliness and frustration; teeny-bop music is less physical than cock-rock, drawing on older, romantic, ballad conventions . . .

Boys, who are interested in rock as music, want to be musicians, technicians, experts. It is boys who form the core of the rock audience, become rock critics and collectors (girl rock fanatics become, by contrast, photographers) . . .

For girls, as for boys, music is background, something to kiss and make up to, but it is also background to a different set of activities and involves different sorts of commitment. Working-class girls, for example, dance more and usually better than boys who (except in specific dancing cults like mod and disco) don't actually dance much at all. Girls buy and practice to dance records (which become part of girl group life) and start dancing much younger . . . Music and musical idols provide a focus for female fantasies just as pop and film stars did for their mothers and grandmothers . . .

**Source 4.7a** (S. Frith, *Sound Effects*)

THINGS YOU DIDN'T KNOW ABOUT BEN

1. When he was six he was in a commercial for Kodak.

2. His first (unrequited) love was Michael Crawford's daughter. "I sent her flowers and really wooed her," he says. "But she wasn't interested."

3. The wallpaper in his bedroom is "lots of shades, of blue. It's got all these flowers, which makes it sound horrid but it isn't. It's like the sea."

4. His favoured underwear is boxer shorts. "Nothing fancy though — just plain grey cotton ones."

5. During his modelling days he once had to play Boy George's lips for the video of *Love Is Love* (a song from the film *Electric Dreams*).

6. His favourite person at school was the biology teacher "because he was tough, but not power mad."

7. His favourite food is an Indian cracker called a poppadom.

8. Ben's first fisherman's hat was chewed up by a friend's dog "when I left it by a pool when we were doing underwater shots for a video. I kept all the bits for sentimental reasons."

9. The rest of Curiosity have nicknamed him Dirty Ben, because he has a bit of a reputation for being a . . . er 'ladies man!'

10. The things he enjoys most in life are eating, fishing, and lying in the bath. "I also love going to night clubs and dancing."

**Source 4.7b** (*My Guy*, 31 Oct. 1987)

## Gender and physical representation

In modern society, it is still common to find that females are more often judged by their physical appearance than other qualities they may possess. Beauty contests typify this attitude. Although the BBC no longer cover the *Miss World* contest, much of the media still place a great emphasis on a woman's looks, e.g. page 3 of the *Sun* and other papers.

### Source 4.8

1. Why have women's bodies been used in these adverts? (Compare the Fiat to the Peugeot advert on page 12).
2. Why do you think male bodies are rarely used in adverts other than with products for the body such as clothes and aftershave?

*Source 4.8a*

PILKINGTON MAKES OVER 20% OF THE WORLD'S FLAT GLASS. SOMETHING THAT'S EASILY IGNORED.

*Source 4.8b*

With a bubbly personality and striking looks to match, *Emmerdale Farm* actress Malandra Burrows – pictured right with Ian Sharrock, who plays Jackie Merrick – should have no problem attracting boyfriends in real life. But Malandra is finding just the opposite applies. As Woolpack barmaid Kathy Bates she is getting engaged to Jackie Merrick this week, and the happy couple are featured on our cover and overpage.

But the blonde, blue-eyed actress, who was 22 earlier this month, confesses that her hectic life revolves around the ITV serial and leaves little time for off-screen romance. 'I have to admit that becoming engaged to Jackie Merrick this week is some compensation,' she says.

The problem is not a lack of boyfriends but her busy rehearsal and filming schedule, combined with the public attention that a regular screen role brings. 'It's a question of having the time to let a relationship develop,' says Malandra.

'And when people come up to me because they recognise me from *Emmerdale*, I enjoy it. But boyfriends have found it difficult to cope with this situation because of the pressure it imposes.

'At the moment, there is no one special in my life, but I have so little time that I can rarely manage even to get back home to see the family in Liverpool. Still, I'm not complaining, especially as I am enjoying *Emmerdale* so much and my role is opening up. If Jackie Merrick and I do marry, you can bet it won't all be plain-sailing.'

Malandra is still staying in the same Yorkshire bed-and-breakfast house near the television studios that she started using more than two years ago.

'Living out of a suitcase doesn't get me down,' she says. 'In fact, I get spoilt rotten by the landlady.'

**Pulling pints – but not men**

*Source 4.9* (*TV Times*, 14 Nov. 1987)

## Source 4.9

1. In what terms is actress Malandra Burrows described in the *TV Times* profile at the bottom of page 68?
2. If the profile had been of Ian Sharrock, the male character, what terms might have been used to describe him?

## Gender and authority

### Source 4.10

What do these sources suggest about how seriously women's views are treated in the media? Since 1975 on BBC (Angela Rippon), and 1976 on ITV (Anna Ford), women have read the news on television.

'Things are stirring among Chelmsford's new district councillors. Temperatures are sent rising at committee meetings by the eagerly-awaited entrance of delicious Wendy Sealy, newly elected member for Waltham ward. The sexy ex-actress seems to be the petite object of many an admiring glance from the usually sober elder statesmen on the council. On occasions she has attended council appointments recently she has looked quite a dish, wearing bright coloured bandanas round her lovely white neck, beautiful golden ringed hair tumbling down her shoulders, black tights. Any other business?' (Story – complete – in *Chelmsford Newsman Herald*.)

**Source 4.10b** (*Images of Women*, NUJ)

**Sunday Mirror**

20p    December 28, 1980    No. 919

*Three days before the official list*

### YOUR New Year Honours

**SEXY ANNA TOPS POLL**

By REVEL BARKER

LOVELY Anna Ford today wins the title she never wanted — Sex Symbol of 1980.

Britain's men rated the ITN beauty streets ahead of stunners like Sophia Loren, Bo Derek and Debbie Harry.

Anna, 36, has always preferred to be judged on the way she reads the News at Ten rather than her looks.

But was she unhappy at being voted the nation's sexiest lady in an exclusive survey conducted for the Sunday Mirror? Not a bit.

"It's terribly touching, very sweet," said Anna when told the result. "I really am delighted."

**Heroes**

More than 1000 men and women in all parts of Britain took part in the poll to compile YOUR New Year Honours List.

The survey (see Pages 10 and 11) included your top personalities and entertainers of 1980 and comes three days before the official Honours List.

Man of the Year is the Pope and your favourite heroes are the SAS and P.c. Trevor Lock for their part in the Iranian Embassy siege in London in May.

Anna also came third in the Woman Of The Year vote—behind the Queen Mother and The Queen.

"I'm really flattered to be included in a list like that," she said.

Modest Anna said: "I'm on holiday, and just shopping about in jeans. I wouldn't want to be photographed like this."

The picture on the right is the one Anna said she would most like Sunday Mirror readers to see.

Anna explained her ideas on glamour. "There has always been a misunderstanding about my views," she said. "My complaint is that women are always talked about on the basis of how they look.

"You get headlines like 'Man and Blonde Die in Car,' as though the only interesting thing about the woman is her hair, and it's sufficient to describe her as just 'blonde'.

"Women are a lot more interesting than that, and have lots of other facets. I'd like people to recognise it, that's all."

Well, Anna, there's still no doubt you're beautiful. Just see what other famous personalities think of you.

Ex-colleague **Reginald Bosanquet** said: "I find her extremely attractive — physically, intellectually and professionally.

"I am not in the least surprised at the result of the poll. We get on well together and I would have voted for her."

Chat show host **Michael Parkinson** said: "The most attractive woman on television is my wife Mary, the second is Miss Piggy, and the third is Anna Ford."

TV star **Bruce Forsyth** said: "She is most attractive. I particularly like her when she has her hair up. She is a very lovely girl."

Actress **Diana Dors** said: "Many men who watch TV obviously sit there and fantasise about her."

Diana's husband, actor **Alan Lake**, said: "I think she appeals to men's primitive instincts."

Top fashion designer **Bill Gibb** said: "Anna is just terrific, I . . ."

*Turn to Page 4.*

*Anna Ford—she chose this picture*

**Happy New Year Anna and to ALL our readers**

**Source 4.10a**

An example from an afternoon DJ show on BBC Radio London (Thursday 30 April):

| | |
|---|---|
| *man presenter:* | But right now, looking as beautiful as ever, it's . . . Oh aren't you nice.ha ha. Hello. Well, old flatterer that I am, yes indeed, I've forgotten what you're going to talk about today. Er yes of course, fruit and veg time isn't it? |
| *woman presenter:* | That's right, yes. We've had lots of nasty weather . . . |
| *man presenter:* | Let's just talk about you and forget the fruit and veg. |
| *woman presenter:* | I'm sure no one's interested in me. |
| *man presenter:* | Yes they are, yes. Alright, we'd better talk about fruit and veg. |
| *woman presenter:* | 'Cos it's quite sad really, we've had some quite nasty frosty weather all over the country . . . It's destroyed all the blossom on the English cherry trees and pear trees, so of course . . . |
| *man presenter:* | Has it interfered with your *pears* then? |
| *woman presenter:* | Yes it might do later on in the year. These things show later on in the year. We shall have to see, won't we? |
| *man presenter:* | Your *pears* show later on in the year do they? |
| *woman presenter:* | Yes they do. |
| *man presenter:* | Yes, because of the cold weather is it? |

**Source 4.10c** (Local Radio Workshop, *Nothing Local About It*, Comedia/Methuen, 1983)

## Gender and work

**1.** *Women's magazines*
Women's magazines have undergone several changes since the war. Margorie Ferguson examined how they had changed between 1949–1974 in *Forever Feminine*. She found that the main theme in the 1950s weeklies was 'getting and keeping your man', especially in the short stories. Gradually, the theme of 'self help' appeared – either in the form of being a better mother, lover, worker, cook, etc., or through overcoming misfortune such as divorce or illness.

By the mid 1970s, women doing paid work outside the home had become a major concern. Magazines like *Cosmopolitan* were promoting the role of 'independent women' capable of earning their own living, and being sexually adventurous. However, Marjorie Ferguson found that throughout the period, the magazines still concentrated on 'him, home and looking good'.

Recently launched magazines like *Prima, Essentials* and *Best* seem to be placing the emphasis back once more on women's traditional domestic activities like sewing, cooking, staying beautiful, etc.

*Source 4.11*  *Woman's Realm,* 1958
How do these extracts from *Woman's Realm* of 1958 contrast with the content of such magazines today? Try to use *Woman, Woman's Realm* or *Woman's Own* as a comparison.

---

### Something to talk about

**by Vera Wynn Griffiths**
*Esmé had always longed to be the stay-at-home wife; but leisure had unexpected disadvantages*

Esmé went out to the car to see David off to work.

'D'you know, this is the first time I've really felt like your wife,' she said excitedly.

'I must say I like that!' he said with a grin, 'considering you've been my wife for three years now.'

'Oh, I know, but – it's just – well never mind, it would take too long to explain now. Goodbye, come

---

### May I help you?
### asks Clare Shepherd

*If you want a reply by post, please enclose a 3d. stamp. Address your letters to Clare Shepherd, Women's Realm, 189 High Holborn, London, W.C.1. You can be sure that letters either for publication or to be answered privately will be treated confidentially, and that your identity will not be disclosed.*

**Q. My sister, who is about five years older than me, has been engaged to a very charming young man for the past three years. They want to get married, but they cannot find anywhere to live.**

**I am very fond of my sister's fiancé, who has always acted like a brother to me, but recently his behaviour has changed, and he has tried flirting with me. Once or twice he has even kissed me rather passionately.**

**I don't want to hurt my sister by telling her this, but I do want to stop this kind of behaviour. What do you suggest?**

**A.** The best thing to do is to see as little of this young man as you can manage without comment. Don't change so markedly as to arouse suspicion in your sister's mind. Also tell the young man that you are certainly not going to betray your sister.

I expect the long engagement has proved trying for both of them, and the sooner they can be married the better. In the meantime, I am glad to find that you are being sensible, and not taking this young man's flirtation seriously. You yourself, I feel, should be getting out more, and meeting young folk of both sexes.

**Q. My girl has told me she never wants to see me again. We had been going steady for six months, and we planned to be married. Then she began to grow distant, and we had our first quarrel when she told me she didn't want me to take her home to her digs. I love her as much as ever.**

**Yesterday I waited for her on her way to the office, but, as soon as she saw me, she crossed the road. I went over to speak to her, and we had a dreadful scene right there in the street. I cannot understand why she has changed so.**

**A.** You know better than I can whether there was any reason for this change in your fiancée. As you say that your first quarrel arose from her refusal to let you take her home, I am wondering whether you perhaps forced physical attentions on her when she was not ready for

Source 4.11a (Woman's Realm, 1958)

home early.'

She stood waving until the car was round the corner, then turned back indoors, into the kitchen where the breakfast dishes were stacked. After washing up, she thought she'd turn out the spare bedroom and wash the curtains; then she'd make a ginger cake. David loved ginger cake and there hadn't been time to make one lately; and some time this morning she'd have a look at her cacti which she kept in the little glass-fronted porch.

The day stretched before her in long, blissful emptiness. There was time for everything now. This afternoon she'd go into town and do some shopping; not hurried shopping for two chops and the necessary groceries, but the sort of shopping when you pottered about looking into windows, drifting into the market, really choosing food. And tonight supper wouldn't be cold ham and a tomato and a bite of cheese. She'd make a bacon and egg pie and a lemon soufflé to follow . . .

The clock chimed half-past eight and here she was still in an apron and slippers. On every other weekday morning during her three years of marriage, she had been properly dressed by this time; face done, hair done, tearing down the road to catch the bus which would take her to the school. That was what she'd meant when she told David that for the first time she felt like his wife. This was the very first morning that she'd been able to stand on the doorstep and wave him off. Always until now, there had been that ghastly rush, both of them getting ready, swallowing some breakfast, trying to get the dishes done so that they wouldn't be there facing them in the evening.

---

them, perhaps when you were wishing her good night. Of course, I may be quite wrong in this assumption, but the more you love your girl the stronger will be your desire for physical expression. This is natural and is nothing to be ashamed of – but all the same, you are the person who should protect your girl from doing anything she may regret.

She may just have found that she does not love you as much as she thought she did. If this is the case, I am afraid you will just have to grin and bear it. You are not the first person who has loved in vain and it is far better that your girl should find she has made a mistake before marriage rather than after. She is within her rights in refusing to have anything more to do with you and you should accept this and avoid any further scenes. If this behaviour is just a tantrum, she is far more likely to come back to you if you respect her wishes now.

**Q. Most parents seem to worry when their teenage children begin to take an interest in the opposite sex. My problem is just the opposite. I have a daughter of sixteen who is still at school. She is very intelligent and her teacher thinks she may get a scholarship for further study.**

**Her father and I are very pleased about this, but I am worried about her because she seems to be far too serious for her age. She has no close friends and takes no interest in boys. Am I worrying unnecessarily?**

**A.** It is rather unnatural for a girl of sixteen to show no interest in boys, but don't forget that some girls develop later than others, and that there is no way you can force her interest.

You could try to make her more sociable by encouraging her to bring friends home. If she has a room of her own, you might help her to entertain her friends in it by turning it into a bed-sitter, and encouraging her to give tea or light supper parties. Adolescents of your daughter's age are often shy of meeting their friends in the company of their parents.

If this plan works, you might then suggest a party with boys among the guests. All that will be necessary will be a gramophone and a few rock 'n' roll records, a room to dance in, and some light refreshments. Though you may not care for rock 'n' roll, it does take the starch out of boys and girls who are otherwise inclined to be stand-offish and shy.

Finally, do make sure that your daughter has becoming clothes, a good hair-style – and as a special present why not let her have a lesson in make-up.

Source 4.11b (Woman's Realm, 1958)

**Source 4.12**

What ideas about women and work do these two adverts represent?

## Rosie the Riveter

Women's place in the workforce was radically changed by WWII. New popular images in propaganda, like 'Rosie the Riveter' were used to recruit women to fill war-time defence jobs which suffered from the 'man' power shortage caused by the war. Black women, along with older and married women, for the first time found exciting new opportunities open to them in non-traditional, skilled and highly paid jobs. Nearly 20 million women were active in the workforce during the war, 6.5 million for the first time. The number of women in heavy manufacturing increased 460%. Overnight, women were trained to be shipbuilders, welders, riveters, and machine workers. In addition, they became the train conductors, bus drivers, lumberjacks and police which sustained the nation. When WWII came to an end, new

propaganda was produced which encouraged women to leave the workforce so the returning soldiers could resume their old jobs. Although women were laid off in great numbers, 80% of them wanted to keep their skilled jobs, and many of the 'Rosies' stayed in the workforce, but were forced to return to their traditional unskilled positions.

**Source 4.12a**

*Source 4.12 b*

**2.** *Television: Cagney and Lacey*
In the television police series of the 1960s and 1970s, the main characters were nearly always male. Series often focused on two males working together (e.g. *Starsky and Hutch, The Sweeney*).

*Source 4.13*   Cagney and Lacey

1. How does this representation of women in police series differ from what you normally see on television and in films?
2. Why do you think it is unusual for two women to be represented as the main characters, especially in their professional work?
3. How important is it for such female characters to be physically attractive?

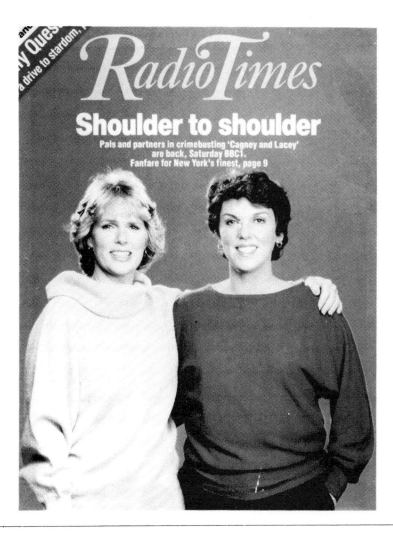

RadioTimes

**Shoulder to shoulder**

Pals and partners in crimebusting 'Cagney and Lacey' are back, Saturday BBC1. Fanfare for New York's finest, page 9

### Cops with a touch of class

*(Cagney and Lacey Appreciation of the Series Society)*
Enthusiasts love the stars because they have obviously not spent all day applying lip gloss. In fact, Christine and Mary Beth can be appealingly frumpy, sometimes wearing quite unflattering clothes. Tyne Daly carried on filming throughout her own pregnancy, which was mirrored in the script; and after the birth she appeared not to have immediately shed those extra pounds, much to the delight of her public. 'At last – a normal-shaped woman,' says Wendy Phillips, herself a successful illustrator who shares a passion for the series with her husband (the fan clubs are 40 per cent male).

The rapport between the two central characters is particularly appealing – such a close and honest friendship is more often portrayed between men. Cagney, the ambitious, abrasive and sometimes lonely single career woman, is the perfect foil to Lacey, who divides her time between work and family commitments.

The 'supporters' have been through a lot with their heroines. Mary Beth Lacey survived breast cancer in an earlier series (narrowly avoiding a mastectomy), only to suffer a gunshot wound a few episodes later. Cagney's pregnancy scare was another cliffhanger: she was just getting to like the idea of pregnancy when the urine test (which viewers saw her carry out on her coffee table) turned out to be negative. 'Women were in tears all across Britain that night,' says Wendy.

It's not only the 'real-life' vulnerability of these characters, and the changes of their professional and emotional lives, that engages people like Tina and Wendy. The programme also reflects and stimulates discussion on such important social issues as racism, abortion, drunken driving and child abuse.

As professionals themselves, Tina and Wendy identify with Cagney and Lacey's dedication to their work, and applaud the fact that they haven't become surrogate men in the process. Says Tina, 'No one's ever acknowledged that you can go into the ladies' room and talk about make-up and period pains and still be serious about work the next minute.'

*Source 4.13*

## Gender representation and production

As can be seen in source 4.14, there are relatively few women involved in media production. Until the 1970s, there had only been a handful of women film directors in Hollywood and Britain. It is only recently that a woman has been employed as an editor of a national newspaper – *News of the World* in 1987.

### Source 4.14

What effects are these inequalities in the number of men and women producing television programmes and newspapers likely to have?

### Activity

Select three or four examples of one area of media production such as a television situation comedy or Sunday national newspaper, and list the number of male and female contributors. On television the credits are given at the beginning or end of a programme, and often appear in *The Radio* or *TV Times* (over half the *Cagney and Lacey* programmes have had women as co-producers). Newspaper journalists are usually named in the main stories. Pop music producers and writers are named on the record, and sometimes the record sleeve.

### Who are the journalists?

Who writes the copy inevitably influences the story it tells.

Roger Smith, who did a significant amount of research on behalf of the NUJ's Equality Working Party (now the Equality Council) came to the conclusion that male domination of the personnel in the national press is a fundamental obstacle to improving the way in which women are portrayed by it.

The research, which was begun nearly ten years ago now, revealed that the number of women journalists was growing. The number of female recruits to local newspapers rose from 23 per cent to 36 per cent in 1975/76. The NUJ's Annual General Report of 1982 also shows that the proportion of qualified women journalists rose from 15 per cent in 1972 to 21 per cent by the end of 1977. The current membership of the NUJ is 23,394 men compared with 9,273 women.

Women with real decision-making power on newspapers are today still very few in number. Many of the largest Fleet Street newspapers, in terms of both staff and circulation, have no women in senior positions at all. Even those with the title of editor within a specialism do not tend to have any executive rank.

Almost four out of every five women are concentrated at the bottom of the organisational hierarchy as news reporters, feature writers and women's page writers. They constitute 10 per cent of general news reporters but the tendency is to relegate them to human-interest type stories rather than 'hard news'.

**Source 4.14a** (TUC, *Images of Inequality,* March 1984).

**Source 4.14b** (BBC Equal Opportunities Office) (ACTT); Post occupancy by sex in British television (*The Listener*, 20 Aug. 1987); BBC employment figures for 1987; ITV employment figures for 1987

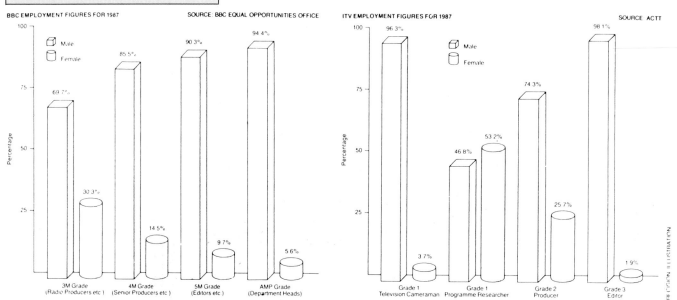

## Gender representation and audience

One of the few television series where women have been represented as independent, and often stronger than men, is soap opera (for further discussion, see pages 93–97). This has much to do with the fact that soap operas have traditionally had larger female audiences, especially during the daytime. The need to take into account female audiences helps to explain why representations of women have changed in recent years.

### Source 4.15

NB: Source 4.15c is on page 76.

1. Why have representations of women in adverts changed, according to David Lipsey?
2. To what extent do the adverts here represent 'new independent' women?
3. How might a 'new man' be represented?

*Cheeky Charlie*

**Charlie** cosmetics and fragrance

C · H · A · R · L · I · E

*Source 4.15a*

Every woman needs her Daily Mail.

So you're not just a good listener at parties.

So you always have a picture of the changing scene.

So, in the evenings, you can tell him a few things he may have been too busy to learn during the day.

So you can keep an eye on how your taxes are being spent.

So you know every day what the famous and infamous are doing and saying.

So you can interrupt your hairdresser once in a while.

So you can increase the children's awareness of the world around them.

So you look forward to the times when you're alone.

So you know, not only who won or lost, but how they played the game.

So you're not just another pretty face.

*Source 4.15b*

## Women in adverts

It is inconceivable now that a British advertiser would dare to screen that frightful Shredded Wheat advert, in which a housewife sang of her duties to the 'two men in my life' (husband, son). Commercials, generally, show women as cool and capable; in charge, and often funny, as in the lady dealing with her McEwen Export-drinking husband and his dummy . . .

Women's power in advertisements has changed because their commercial power has changed.

There are now a million single-parent families, roughly double the 1971 proportion. In more and more families, the woman is involved in purchasing decisions. Some women are now well-off in their own right. And with these changes in the marketplace have gone more changes in attitudes. Fewer and fewer people believe that a woman's place is in the home.

These changes are not the product of advertising; advertisers never take the lead. But they have – more or less willingly – accommodated themselves to change. Indeed, crude calculations of self-interest have dictated that they must adapt, or lose customers.

**Source 4.15 c**  (D. Lipsey, *New Society,* 21 Aug, 1987)

# Representations of race/ethnicity

There are many stereotypes of people on the basis of their ethnic group (i.e. their shared national culture).

**Source 4.16**
Which two ethnic stereotypes are represented in this source?

---

**Activity**

Make a list of stereotypes for the following groups:
**a.** Irish
**b.** Welsh
**c.** Scots
**d.** English
**e.** Italians
**f.** French
**g.** Germans
**h.** Australians
**i.** Americans
**j.** Japanese
**k.** Iranians
1.  For which of the above groups have you found it **a.** easiest, **b.** hardest, to think of stereotypes?
2.  Why is it so easy or difficult to think of stereotypes for these groups?

---

Media representations of ethnic groups, and people from other countries in general, vary from the exotic and interesting, to the strange and threatening. Where ideas support the view that our culture is superior to others, then this is called **ethnocentrism**. Where ideas support the belief that other people are inferior, then this is called **racism**. Racism has tended to draw on physical differences between people, especially skin colour. Such beliefs can be traced back to colonial rule in the case of Britain. It is easier to dominate and exploit people when it is thought (falsely) that they are less developed or more primitive.

---

### 'Allo 'Allo!
### Saturday 7.20
### BBC1

YOU ARE probably wondering what I am doing here backstage at the Prince of Wales theatre. Well, I am talking to Gorden Kaye and the gang from the Café René. And, yes, I am listening very carefully.

As the fourth series of 'Allo 'Allo! makes the airwaves crackle. it's time to check up on the sauce at the café of laughs. The whole caboodle has crossed the Channel and taken up occupation in one of London's most prestigious theatres.

'I 'ave 'eard of your Arthur Daley,' Gorden says. "E is a vairy clever man. What we call in France an *entrepreneur* ('ow you call eet in English?) I 'ave a plan. There are so many legless frogs about, I'd 'ave a nice leetle earner making leetle crutches for them.'

**Source 4.16a**  (*Radio Times,* 7 Nov. 1987)

**Source 4.16b**  Fawlty Towers (BBC Enterprises Limited 1979)

**Figure 4.2**  (P. Oliver, *The Story of the Blues*, Penguin, 1972)

The 'screaming idiotic words and savage music' – then called rhythm and blues – later became known as rock and roll, and is still the basis for today's rock/pop music enjoyed by people throughout the western world.

### Source 4.17

How do these two images differ in their representation of black people?

It would seem that compared to older Hollywood images of black people as simple and fun loving, such as in *Gone with the Wind*, modern images are more likely to portray blacks on a par with whites, such as in American television series like *Hill Street Blues* or *The Cosby Show*. Although there are more positive images of black people today, much depends on the **context** of media representations. Stereotyping may be simply more subtly constructed, many of the old assumptions still exist, and new ones have developed.

**Source 4.17a**  Bob Hope and Willie Best in *The Ghost Breakers*.

Dateline America

by Lesley Salisbury
in Hollywood

Left: Bill Cosby with
Keshia Knight Pulliam,
who plays screen
daughter Rudy, filming
'The Cosby Show'
in Hollywood.

**Source 4.17b**  (*TV Times*, 21 Nov. 1987)

## Race and the news

*Source 4.18*

1. What do these images and headlines say about blacks in Britain?
2. Would the label white be applied to the stories if white people had been involved?
3. What terms might black people use to describe their actions instead of 'thug', 'prowling West Indian', and 'race terror'?

Few journalists set out to stir up racial hatred. Part of the explanation for such reporting is that it is based on news values of drama, threat, spectacle, etc. (as discussed on pages 51–2) in an attempt to boost circulation or ratings. Little space exists for background explanation, such as the long term effects of poverty, conflict with the police and racial harassment. Furthermore, most journalists are white and reflect the views of the dominant cultural group in society. The views of minority groups rarely get voiced, because very few are employed within the media and they lack right of access.

**THE Sun**

**BLITZ ISSUE**
Pages 2, 3, 4, 5, 6, 14 & 15

Wednesday, September 11, 1985          18p          TODAY'S TV: PAGE 12

## HATE OF A BLACK BOMBER

**By IAN HEPBURN, who was attacked by the mob**

A BLACK thug stalks a Birmingham street with hate in his eyes and a petrol bomb in his hand.

The prowling West Indian was one of the hoodlums who brought new race terror to the city's riot-torn Handsworth district yesterday.

And as darkness fell over the smoke-blackened ruins of a stunned community, fresh violence flared last night as hundreds of police in riot gear faced gangs hurling bottles and stones.

More fires were started, and there were several arrests.

At least two innocent Asians have died and 45 shops have been burnt out and looted in the riots.

Last night police forces all over Britain were put on red alert in case "copy-cat" violence flares in their areas. In Toxteth, Liverpool, officers were drafted into the area in armoured vehicles.

THUG . . . a prowling petrol-bomber hunts for a target in riot-torn Handsworth

*Source 4.18a*

**2 CHANCES TO WIN A FORTUNE**
Pages 40 & 43

**DAILY EXPRESS**

Friday November 6 1987          ★★★          22p

ANGER AS POLICE BOSS RAPS COLOURED MUGGERS

# YARD CHIEF IN BLACKS CRIME ROW

By JOHN COLES

THIS WAS YOUR LIFE—DAILY EXPRESS TRIBUTE: PAGES 4 & 5

*Source 4.18b*

## Third World images

The further away a foreign culture or country is the less it is likely to feature within the British media. This is particularly true of Third World countries, a label used to apply to poorer, less industrialised countries in Africa, Asia and Latin America. It usually requires something very dramatic to happen, such as a war or natural disaster, before such countries are mentioned in news or current affairs coverage.

*Source 4.19*

1. How do each of these images represent Africa?
2. Why do they seem inconsistent?
3. Where are you likely to find such images in the media?
4. How might they affect ideas and attitudes towards black people in Britain?

*Source 4.19b*   (*New Internationalist,* May 1986)

*Source 4.19c*

*Source 4.19a*   (*Ten 8* no. 19, 1985)

## Multicultural representations

This means reflecting the fact that Britain is made up of more than one culture – i.e. ways of life, religions, customs and beliefs.

*Source 4.20*  A multicultural plot
How far might providing separate programmes on television for different ethnic minorities help to overcome racial and ethnic stereotyping in television as a whole?

*Source 4.20*  (*Television and Radio*, IBA, 1988)

**Above:** *Division of Hearts,* part of the programming associated with the 40th anniversary of Indian/ Pakistani/Bangladeshi independence, tells the story through the eyes of the ordinary people of the sub-continent.

Part of Channel 4's brief was to provide programmes 'for all of the people some of the time'.

 Channel 4 presently has at least 35 companies producing programmes with 'multicultural' content all over the schedule. They comprise teams of people from ethnic minority backgrounds, mostly in creative partnership with people who do not have such a background. In some cases it is just one black or Asian writer working with a black director and a white production team. In other instances, editors, researchers and technical personnel from Asian, Afro-Caribbean or Chinese backgrounds are working with equally skilled people sympathetic to the style and content of what they want to bring to the screen. In this way a sector which is in no sense 'ghettoised' has been constructed.

*IBA Television and Radio 1988*

## Representations of
## social class

What do we mean by social class?

*Source 4.21*
What do these magazine contents
tell you about differences in social
class?

PAGE 3

# Contents

EDITOR: Brian Lee     CIRCULATION: Bill Wilson
ADVERTISEMENT MANAGER: Henry Hicks, 01-353
8522/01-353 6000 ext. 767
TITBITS' ADDRESS: Northcliffe House, London
EC4Y OJA.

*Source 4.21b*   (*Titbits*, Dec.
1987)

# CONTENTS

*Source 4.21a*   (*Good Housekeeping*, Dec. 1987)

**Source 4.22**

Contrast these two representations of social class.

Social class is based on inequalities in wealth and income, and differences in lifestyle and attitudes. These might be apparent in newspapers (e.g. comparing the *Financial Times* and the *Sun*) and magazines, but what of broadcasting? Television and radio would claim to be classless. Whilst programmes are aimed at mass audiences, there are differences in the way classes are represented.

## Cuddle up with Clarence

'He's a lovely teddy bear of a man,' says Ronnie Barker, speaking not of himself but of **Clarence** (Monday BBC2), the clumsy, cockney removal man who is his latest TV persona. Clarence takes a sudden fancy to an equally unglamorous, middle-aged ladies' maid (Josephine Tewson) and sets up house with her in the country.

*Source 4.22a*   (*Radio Times*, 2 Jan. 1988)

☐*ITV: A Royal G*

# Choosir

continued from page 29 from the room. The Quee likes to make this strictly family affair.

The reason for exchanging gifts on Christmas Eve dates back to Queen Alexandra's time. Edward VII's wife was born in Denmark, where people open their presents the night before Christmas.

After this opening ceremony, most of the treasures are left on display on the table, but the children race off around the castle, trying

*Buying and receiving Christmas gifts is as much fun for the Royal Family as for anyone else. Above: the Princess of Wales loves shopping sprees. Above, right: any present connected with fishing will keep Prince Charles happy. Right: the Duke of York likes to give his flamboyant Duchess hats as gifts.*

*Source 4.22b*   (*TV Times*, 19 Dec. 1987)

Social class may affect the media in so far as those with most power (the upper and middle classes) are more likely to own, control or be in a position to exert influence. Those with most authority in society – leading politicians, judges, company directors, royalty, etc., tend to have their views treated seriously. Their opinions carry weight in the media, so they have the ability to *set the agenda* for the issues that are discussed. Poorer, less powerful groups have more difficulty drawing attention to what may concern them.

One media research group, the Glasgow University Media Group have found that during strikes, management views are likely to be given more prominence than those of trade unions or workers, not only in the press but on television. For example, employers or managers are usually interviewed alone in their office which is in contrast to workers who are often shown outside or as part of a noisy group. The employers are reported as making *offers* whereas workers or unions are making *demands*. Strong management action is described as firm, whilst workers actions are described as militant. The cost of strikes (i.e. lost production and wages) are nearly always attributed to the workers on strike, rather than be blamed on employers or the government, and so on.

---

**The Queen, A Royal Year, The Queen & the Commonwealth    C4: The Old Man of Lochnagar**

## presents for the family that has everything

*Presents for outdoor types suit the Duke of York and Duke of Edinburgh (above). The Queen Mother (right) receives gifts of little luxuries from her loved ones.*

out new toys or showing them off to everyone.

The Queen likes to give books – non-fiction, thrillers or biographies to Prince Charles and her husband. The Duke of York gets the latest technical books on photography and, in exchange, he often gives his mother a framed photograph he has taken himself.

Close friends often receive yet another book

on breeding dogs or bloodstock from the Queen. She is not so keen on burying her nose in a book herself, so relatives usually give her dog leads, headscarves, or photograph albums.

One Christmas, she received a pair of porcelain candlesticks as her main gift from the Prince and Princess of Wales. But, when the Prince filled a stocking for his mother – the way he

has done ever since he was a teenager – the Princess popped in some corgi-shaped soaps she had bought from Crabtree & Evelyn in Kensington.

Princess Anne likes practical gifts and once

asked a member of her staff to make sure that Prince Charles gave her the doormat she needed for her home at Gatcombe Park. In return, she knows he always loves receiving any kind of fishing tackle.

The Queen Mother is

known to love little luxuries, so the Princess of Wales gave her a pale-blue swansdown powder-puff two years ago.

Prince Edward's interest in the theatre guarantees that he will get new books *continued on page 33*

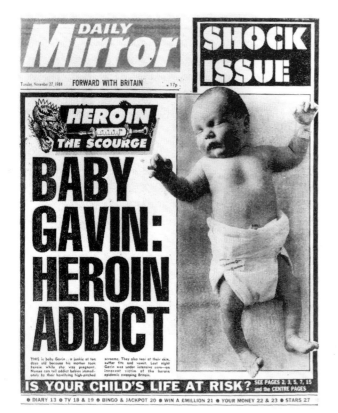

*Source 4.23a*

*Source 4.23b*

### Childhood

Until this century, most children did not have a special status in society. In fact, they were seen as miniature adults, who would usually work and contribute to the family as soon as physically possible. We now see children very differently.

*Source 4.23*

1. What do these images represent about childhood?
2. Look at the image of the child in source 4.19 (page 79). Why are the cameramen focusing on the child?

> **Activity**
>
> From eight television adverts featuring babies and young children, make a content analysis of how they are represented. Note their expression, voice, activity, the setting and which adults (if any) are present. Why have they been chosen for the advert?

*Source 4.24a*

## Youth

**Source 4.24**

1. How do these representations of youth differ?
2. Explain how each might be used within the media.

# John Craven's BACK PAGES BACK PAGES BACK PAG

Mr Cowan v Gillian, Mr Jones v Sophie and Miss Sangster v Jonathon.
Who will win the trophy that quizmaster Bruno is looking after?

## Seeing things

IN 1967, when he wrote **Ernie's Incredible Illucinations** (Wednesday 5.10 BBC1), Alan Ayckbourn hadn't yet become a famous playwright.

He says that he wrote it to be performed by, and for, children of around 11 and 12 years old, because, at the time, no one seemed to be writing plays for that particular age group.

The trouble with Ernie's 'illucinations' is that everyone else, including Dad (above) experiences them too. Chaos reigns.

# Who'll be top of the class?

SIX OF THE BEST – that's what quizmaster Bruno Brookes calls the finalists in **Beat the Teacher** (Monday 4.40, Tuesday and Wednesday 4.15, Thursday 4.20 BBC1) and by the end of the last programme one of them will be the champion of champions.

Battling it out will be Sophie Mainstone and Mr Jones on Monday; Jonathon Cameron and Miss Sangster on Tuesday; and Gillian Desborough and Mr Cowan on Wednesday. Pupil and teacher with highest points qualify for Thursday's final.

*Sophie:*
Beaminster Comprehensive School. She played four games, winning a total of 630 points. Her hobbies are swimming, disco dancing and collecting frogs. Says Bruno, 'now's her chance to get even with Mr Jones, who beat her earlier on'.

*Mr Jones:*
Jordanthorpe School, Sheffield. Maths master, played nine games with a total of 1,600 points and won a portable music centre/TV and a cassette player. 'He's quite a heart-throb,' says Bruno, 'but girls needn't write in – he got engaged during the series!'

*Jonathon:*
Macclesfield County High School. Unbeaten after nine games, with a total of 1,900 points. He likes sports, fishing and watching TV. Prizes include a camera, keyboards and a portable music centre/TV. Bruno's verdict: 'A real whiz kid.'

*Miss Sangster:*
Eastholm School, Peterborough. PE teacher, played three games for 520 points. She likes cooking, gardening, piano-playing. 'She's determined, in a nice way,' says Bruno.

*Gillian:*
Charles Darwin School, Biggin Hill. Played three games, gained 570 points. Loves trekking through the countryside on her horse. 'She can pounce on the points at just the right moment,'says Bruno.

*Mr Cowan:*
Rhyll High School. Teaches English, history and general studies, and picked up 400 points from three games. Bruno thinks Mr Cowan could give lessons on how to win on *Beat the Teacher* –'he's a really good sport.'

The finals have lots of the features that became big favourites as well as some specially-devised activity rounds. And there'll be clips from pop videos and cartoons in the observation contest. 'It's all going to be very close,' predicts Bruno, 'and anyone could win.'

**Source 4.24b**   (*Radio Times*, 7 Nov. 1987)

## BRAINBOX by Clive Doig

### FOOTBALL

Five teams played each other once. Scoring two points for a win, one for a draw, the final table looked like this:

| TEAM | GOALS FOR | GOALS AGAINST | POINTS |
|------|-----------|---------------|--------|
| Minty | aa | a | b |
| Nontown | b | c | d |
| Oghead | d | e | e |
| Pester | f | g | h |
| Queenford | h | i | a |

The numbers one to nine have been substituted by letters. All the games had different results. Pester lost to Minty 0-5 and to Nontown 0-3. Queenford only scored three goals altogether. Simon Tusker of Oghead was the only player to score a hat trick, and Uriah Valheim of Minty scored in every game. Minty's goalie only once failed to make a save.

If Nontown and Oghead drew 2-2, what was the score in the Minty v Queenford match?

### TRACKWORD

How many words of three letters or more can you find by tracking from one square to the next, going up, down, sideways or diagonally in order? You may not go through the same letter square again in any one word. No plurals, proper nouns or foreign words are allowed. What is the hidden nine-letter word?
Brainbox: 56 words; average: 34

| R | D | D |
|---|---|---|
| A | O | E |
| W | R | F |

Last week's answers – Intertwinables.
SORE and CUB give SCOURED; TREES and HOME give THREESOME; FIND and RELY give FRIENDLY
**Trackword:** OPPORTUNE

**Folk devils** is a term that refers to images of people we should reject. The popular press, in particular, label certain groups as a social problem and in need of control. Youths are often portrayed as folk devils.

*Source 4.25*

1. Who are the folk devils here?
2. Why do you think young people are labelled as folk devils by the press? (See pages 51–2 on news values.)
3. Are there any young folk devils currently appearing in the press?

## Moral panics

Often, within the media, a group of people or type of behaviour come to be seen as a threat to society. This is called a **moral panic**. A campaign develops, usually involving politicians and people in authority, who draw attention to what they think is a problem. Moral panics in the past have been about football hooligans, drug addicts, muggers, glue-sniffers, student rebels, pot-smokers, and recently, AIDS. Each problem is simplified, those blamed are given a bad name, public opinion is whipped up against them, and all this leads to stronger controls by those in authority.

*Source 4.25*

### Activity

See if you can spot a moral panic in the popular press. Try to answer the following questions:

1. What is the problem?
2. Who are identified as the cause?
3. How are they labelled?
4. Whose views in positions of authority are given? e.g. MPs, police, etc.?
5. What suggestions are made for controlling and solving the problem?

## Marketing youth

What may originally be a threatening or shocking image can, over time, become tamed or defused by the media and made into something more safe (and profitable). For example, it was not long before 'punk' style characters began to appear in adverts for such services as opening a bank account.

James Dean is often thought of as one of the first youth rebels. (He died in a car crash in 1956.)

**Source 4.26**
How are these representations of 'rebellious' youth being used?

*Source 4.26a*

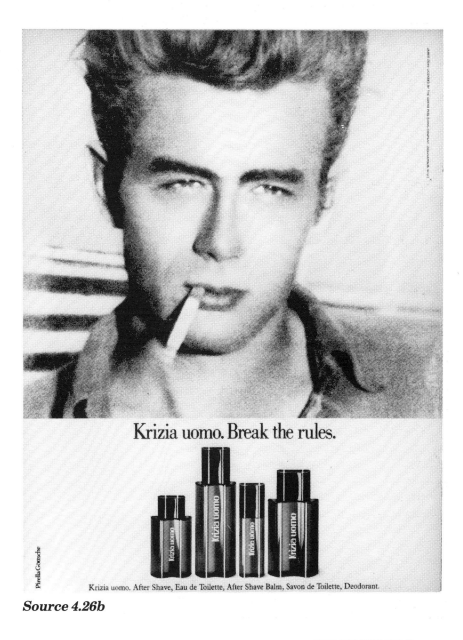

*Source 4.26b*

## Old age

Research into media representations of old age in America and Britain has shown that the elderly (60 and over) are generally viewed rather negatively. A common image is that of the old person as a victim – of violence, deprivation, loneliness, ill health, etc. Discriminating against people on the grounds of their age is referred to as **ageism**.

*Source 4.27*  The image of the elderly on television

1. What does this tell you about the profile of the elderly person most likely to appear on television?
2. Why do you think such differences occur between the numbers of elderly in different categories?
3. Why are the elderly so rarely central characters?

| The image of the elderly on TV | |
| --- | --- |
| Appearances of the elderly (aged 60) on television in Britain in one week of March 1983. | |
| Total number of programmes | 487 |
| Total number of programmes with elderly subjects appearing | 285 |
| Total number of elderly males appearing | 858 |
| Total number of elderly females appearing | 212 |
| Central characters who were elderly males | 251 |
| Central characters who were elderly females | 41 |
| Social class of elderly: | |
| Middle class – Managerial/Professional/ | 87% |
| Clerical | 2% |
| Working class – Manual workers | 10% |
| Unemployed | 1% |

*Source 4.27*  (University of the Third Age in Cambridge, *Research Report No.1*, 1984)

*Source 4.28*  *The Golden Girls*
Why is this description of characters not typical of media representations of the elderly?

**Activity**

1. From the press, collect four stories which feature the elderly.
   How are they represented in each story?
   Why have they been chosen as news stories?
   How are they physically described?
2. Choose five elderly people who regularly appear on television. How often are they represented as:
   a. wise – foolish
   b. comfortable – badly off
   c. fit – unfit
   d. sexually active – inactive
   e. tolerant – intolerant
   f. powerful – powerless
   g. independent – dependent
   h. respected – not respected.

# Estelle reaches her golden age

**W**hen *The Golden Girls* get together each Friday on C4, it's hardly *Listen with Mother* time. They may look like a twittery sewing circle made up of everyone's favourite aunts, mothers and grandmas, but their needles could be sharpened on their tongues.

Topics you'd think would make your granny's perm frizzle are discussed with unflinching regularity: sex (too much and too little), more sex, the pros and cons of dating midgets, drooping breasts, plastic surgery, heart attacks, death, drugs, incontinence, wind, abortion, ex-husbands, hot flushes and funerals.

'It's honest,' says Betty White, who plays sweet, vague, rambling Rose. 'The show's about real life. Probably if young actresses discussed taboo subjects the way we do, the show would be bleeped. They'd be accused of doing it for shock value. But we four ladies have been round the Horn several times. We're having so much fun, it should be illegal. It's nice to know you don't self-destruct after 40.'

The four ladies – Betty, Bea Arthur (Dorothy), Rue McClanahan (Blanche) and Estelle Getty (Sophia) – think the show is, in Rue's words, 'a gift from the gods'. It rescued them from endless bit-parts and *Love Boat* guest-starring roles, has given them sizeable nest-eggs, changed the life of New York-based stage actress Estelle and made them all symbols of success for the over-60s (something that Rue, 52 and a good 10 years younger than her co-stars, bristles at – much like her character Blanche, the desperate divorcee who will be 30 till the day she dies).

**Source 4.28**   (*TV Times*, 7 Nov. 1987)

# 5 GENRE

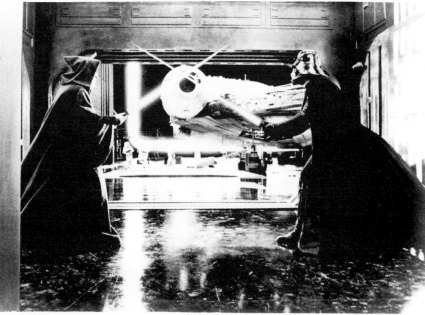

**Source 5.1a**

**Source 5.1b**

*Source 5.1*  Film genre
These two pictures are taken from films.

1. What kind of films are they?
2. What sort of themes and plots are likely to occur?
3. Which characters would you expect to appear?
4. Where is the action likely to take place?
5. What are typical titles of such films?

When similar types of films, television programmes, music, etc. are grouped together they are referred to as **genre**. They are thought to have common codes and conventions.

Consider the example of the **western** in films. It is traditionally recognised by the following:

1. Narrative – themes of revenge, law and order, civilising the west.
2. Main characters – sheriff, gunfighter, pioneer, cavalry, Indians, outlaws, gamblers, judge, etc.
3. Appearance – western clothes i.e. hats, boots; the heroes, in white and clean-shaven, versus the villains, in black and unshaven; the saloon versus pioneer woman.
4. Objects – guns, holsters, horses.
5. Settings – outdoors, plains, deserts, mountains, frontier towns, ranches, forts.

**Activity**

Select one of the following film genres: musical, gangster, science fiction or horror, and write down how each of the headings above applies to that genre.

**Problems with genre categories**

If you compare your list to others, you will find you have noted different aspects. Genres can never be precise categories. As cultural products, films need to be individually distinctive for audiences to enjoy them – unlike industrial products, which are usually made in standardised form. Furthermore, some films may be so original as to be unlike any other, or they may be a cross between different genres.

*Figure 5.1*

*Figure 5.2*

*Source 5.2*
To which genres do these films
belong?

*Source 5.2*

Furthermore, genres are not
static. New examples may
develop the range of themes and
characters. For example, the
1960s ('spaghetti') westerns,
starring Clint Eastwood, were
very different from the John
Wayne westerns of the 1940s and
1950s. The 'hero' of such films
was no longer so clearly in the
right, and the violence became
much more bloody.

**Figure 5.3**   Clint Eastwood in *For a Few Dollars More*

# Television genre

## Activities

1. From a copy of the *Radio Times* and *TV Times* try and identify three genres. Describe what is typical of each genre in terms of:
   a. the setting
   b. the presenters, actors and performers
   c. the themes and plots.
2. Watch (and if possible, record) the *title sequences* which introduce three examples of a genre. Describe any similarities of music, graphics, settings, performers appearing and other information provided about the programme.
3. Find out on which days, at which times of day, and for how long, examples from a genre are likely to be broadcast (i.e. their *scheduling*).
4. Look at the ratings (on page 104). Which genre seems to be the most popular?

## Production and audience

In Chapter 3, it was noted that one of the key factors influencing media production was the need for profit. To achieve this in film and television, production costs must be kept low, and the audience size should be as high as possible.

How might genres enable media companies to make greater profits?

Given the uncertainty of audience tastes (see William Goldman's comments on page 43), and the general decline in cinema audiences, it is not surprising that no genre productions are sure to be successful. Instead, popular films are often made into 'mini genres' in the form of sequels which may be numerous, e.g. *Jaws I–III* and the *Rambo* series. The most popular genre within television is, without doubt, soap opera.

## Soap opera

Soap operas originated in America. The name comes from the fact that the programmes were sponsored by manufacturers of soap powder. Traditional American soap is broadcast daily, unlike in Britain. Here are some summaries of typical daytime soaps.

### Source 5.3

1. How are the plots similar to, and different from British soaps?
2. *Neighbours* is an example of an Australian soap opera which is broadcast on weekdays by the BBC. What differences in plot, themes and characters does it have to *Brookside*, which is also set in a suburban close?

---

### *Here are summaries of last week's soap opera plots*

#### Loving

Isabel confused when Cabot is upset at thought of inviting Shana to dinner. Jim admits to Shana he still has feelings for her but his priestly vows come first. Warren warns Mike he has to see the psychiatrist or he'll be dropped from police force. Lorna, offered job as model, decides to have abortion without telling Tony. Rose unhappy about Stacy dating Curtis. Loran talks her parents into letting Tony and her live at gatehouse and later tells Tony it was her grandparents' idea. Rita Mae finally realizes how much Billy wants a child and agrees to start a family. Suffering writer's block, Doug is going to New York to talk to producer of new play and hopes to regain his writing ability.

#### One life to live

Going against advice of lawyers, Vicki decides to let workers take over plant. When bankers will not give money to workers, Bo/Bill secretly guarantees loan. Tired of living at boarding house, Bo asks to move into O'Neill household. Harry agrees and give him room belonging to Didi, the oldest O'Neill daughter who is away at college. The night Bo/Bill moves into the room, Didi, who has decided to quit school, shows up. Jenny, having decided to break up with David, heads for retreat. Brad appears and she learns that he arranged for Liat to stop wedding ceremony. Feeling totally shattered by Brad's confession, Jenny decides to return to nunnery. Herb, realizing he still loves Dorian, asks her to come home when she is released from hospital and he will help her with paralysis treatment. Herb asked to head commission to halt suburban mob influence. Dee fired by Anthony.

#### Ryan's hope

A drunken Roger makes a phone call to Maggie, who panics. Frank rushes to her side. They share a passionate kiss and Bess is stunned when she discovers

---

***Source 5.3*** (*Cleveland Plain Dealer,* 1 Apr. 1984)

Within soap opera, much of the action takes place in a distinctive area – a street, village or house. There are usually a limited number of characters, whose relationships form the basis for the plot. Part of the pleasure for viewers (or listeners for radio soap opera) is the constant posing of questions – what will happen next? Audiences are frequently left to ponder on how characters will react to a dilemma, or what may happen to them in the next episode. Because each episode ends with stories left unfinished, then the last scene is referred to as a cliffhanger. This can vary from high drama to comic surprise.

Maggie and Frank in Maggie's bed. Bess blames Maggie, but apologizes when she realizes Roger tried to rape Maggie. Roger tells Frank he remembers nothing of the phone call. Fearing he's having alcoholic blackouts, Roger decides to stop drinking, but soon breaks his promise. In Nice, Seneca suggests Jill was happier when she was married to him. Jill angry when Seneca says if Roger keeps drinking, his job is over at the hospital. Johnny becomes furious when he walks in and spots a leotard-clad Katie in the living room with Rick. Pat tells Johnny that Katie's old enough to have boyfriends visit her. Maggie goes on commercial interview and is assured job if she'll sleep with the director. Katie and Maggie talk Dave into turning loft into living quarters for them.

### Search for tomorrow

Feeling he's caused Suzi to leave town, Cagney starts drinking. Warren tells Wendy that Cagney is father of Suzi's child. Sunny insists on return to work but becomes hysterical when she realizes that Jack, who was acquitted of rape charges, is also working at the station. Cagney pays visit to comatose Justine in the hospital and is stunned when he runs into Suzi, who has applied for a job there. Warren horrified to learn share in nightclub he won from Martin is useless as Martin recently sold his interest to Lloyd.

### Young and the restless

Carole tells Jack she wants him to look at her as a woman, not just a friend. Jack fears Carl is aware of the problem he and Jill are having. Lindsay informs Jack his turning his back on her made her become black-mailer. When Diane is offered New York modelling job, Andy offers to leave town with her. Liz worried about Kaye's surgery, while Jill hopes she dies during the face lift. Dina relieved when she thinks Mark is leaving town. Mark gets letter from his sister Danielle, who reminds him they must have revenge on Dina. Tracy upset because whe was unable to make love to Tim.

© *News America Syndicate*

***Source 5.3*** (Continued from page 93)

# On the street where they live...

Over the years – like any other place in Britain – families and familiar faces have moved in and out of Coronation Street, leaving a store of memories. Behind the drawn lace curtains there have been marriage rows and marriage vows, the rustle of chip shop dinners, raised hopes, tales of tragedy and those touches of northern humour that make the world go round. Here, house by house, is the history of the most famous street in the country:

## Rovers Return

Tel: Weatherfield 715 2271
1930–37  George and Elsie Diggins.
1937  Jack and Annie Walker moved in.
1938  Billy Walker was born and, two years later, his sister Joan.
1970  Jack Walker died, leaving Annie to take over the licence.
1984  Annie retired on 8 August. Fred Gee manned the pumps until Billy Walker returned.
1984  December – Billy left and relief manager Gordon Lewis moved in for two weeks.
Temporary manager Frank Harvey then took over until. . .
1985  Bet Lynch was appointed manager on 4 February.

## Number 1

Tel: 715 8827
Present Occupants: Ken and Deirdre Barlow and Tracey.
Previous Occupants:
1920  Albert Tatlock until his death in 1984.
1960–61  Albert's niece Valerie Tatlock (later Barlow).
1972  Ken Barlow.
1981  Deirdre married Ken, and she and Tracey moved in.

## Number 3

Tel: 715 5417
Present Occupants: Emily Bishop and Curly Watts.
Previous Occupants:
1939  Frank and Ida Barlow and their son Ken.
1942  David Barlow born.

1961  Ida was killed in a road accident.
1963  Frank moved to Bramhall, leaving the house empty.
1964  Squatters Betty Lawson and her sons Clifford and Ronnie moved in.
1968–70  Audrey and Dickie Fleming.
1971  Ken Barlow rented the house from Audrey after his wife Valerie's death.
1972  Ken handed the keys over to Ernest and Emily Bishop.

*Source 5.4* (*Coronation Street,* Granada, 1985)

**EastEnders**
**Tuesday and Thursday**
**7.0 BBC1**

Ask any EastEnder for directions to Albert Square, London Borough of Walford, E20, and they'll tell you 'Straight down Turpin Road Market, turn right into Bridge Street, and there it is with the Queen Vic pub on the corner.'

Ask anyone and they'll tell you that the two best-known families in the square are the Beales and the Fowlers. 'Lived here since the year dot!' **Lou Beale**, in her 70s is head of a large cockney family. She's plump, loud, funny and sentimental – but can be stubborn, too.

Two of Lou's children have stayed in the East End: Pauline and Pete – **Pauline Fowler**, who does the morning shift at the local launderette is married to Arther and they have two teenage kids, **Mark** and **Michelle**. They share Lou's house: 45 Albert Square.

Pauline's twin brother, **Pete**, who has a fruit 'n' veg stall in Bridge Street, lives with his second wife, **Kathy**, and son **Ian** in a flat on the nearby 'estate'.

Ask anyone about the Beales and the Fowlers. **Den Watts**, for instance, the guv'nor of the Queen Vic, is Pete Beale's best mate. Pete's barrow is right outside the pub. Since the lads were school kids Den's always been on the fiddle, and Pete's always covered for him. S'what mates are for, innit?

Ask anyone who holds that pub together, and they'll say '*She* does! Angie is no fool.' Lately, the publican's wife is starting to wonder if she's the one who's being 'fiddled' by Jack-the-lad Den. Tricky that, seeing as Angie's best mate is Kathy, Pete's wife, and Kathy doesn't lie. It's all a bit tough on Den and Angie's adopted daughter, **Sharon** – piggy-in-the-middle.

There are not many people in Albert Square **Dr Harold Legg** doesn't know – he brought them into the world. Lou Beale can't work out why he keeps his surgery in the square, as he moved home out of the district years ago. An old-fashioned 'family doctor', he goes back a long way with Lou. He can see right through her and knows when she's being the battleaxe, that it's all an act so that she can get her own way – which is most of the time!

Dr Legg's cleaning lady, **Ethel Skinner**, lives in the flat above the surgery. She's Lou Beale's greatest friend. You can't miss Ethel: she's always wearing a hat and always followed by her little dog, Willy. She also cleans the pub – when she turns up, that is! She's inclined to get carried away telling fortunes in the market or getting conned into doing laundry for Lofty.

**Lofty Holloway** occupies the flat above Ethel. Funny lad, Lofty. He's got the gift of the gab all right, can

Many viewers often react to the lives of soap actors as if they were real people, sending them get well cards, wedding cards, etc. The programme makers seem to go to great lengths to make the end product appear real. For example, in *Brookside*, Mersey Television actually bought real houses for the setting.

*Source 5.5*

*Source 5.5* (*Radio Times*, 16 Feb. 1985)

charm the birds off the trees. But he keeps vanishing – for days on end. Lofty does work now and then. Like three sessions behind the bar at the pub – cash in hand, of course.

**Ali** and **Sue Osman** and nine-month-old baby **Hassan**, live in a council flat in the run-down side of Albert Square. They run Ali's Cafe in Bridge Street, just across the road from the Vic and frequented by the market traders. Ali, a Turkish Cypriot, is likeable but lazy, and gambles away half the cafe's takings, which doesn't keep Sue in the best of moods. She's sharp-tongued at the best of times. And that's what gets up Kathy Beale's nose.

In the room above Sue and Ali's (and sharing the bathroom) is **Mary Smith** and her nine-week-old daughter **Annie**. No one in the square is convinced she is going to be able to manage. Lou says that Mary's a bit young to be bringing up a child alone. Sue Osman reckons she clutters up the bathroom.

Ask anyone if there's a builder, decorator, handyman in the square and they'll point you in the direction of number 3, where **Tony Carpenter** lives. Or *will* live when he finishes 'doing it up'. Meanwhile, he sleeps in his van. Tony is about to get a divorce, and his wife is convinced he won't stay in Walford. Tony has no staying power, she believes.

**Kelvin,** Tony's son, is studying for his GCEs. He could do without the aggro between his parents. He's also got problems with Michelle Fowler and Sharon Watts, the rivals for his affections.

Opposite Al's Cafe is the Foodstore run by two young Bengalis, **Saeed** and **Naima Jeffery,** who live round the corner in the square. Their marriage was hastily arranged because Saeed's parents had to return to India and wanted someone to keep the business going. But shop work is very new and confusing for

them – rather similar to their relationship. If you ask Lou Beale, she will tell you the shop carries 'too much foreign muck'.

And there are newcomers in the square, too. **Debs** and **Andy** are working-class professionals (she works in a bank, he's a children's nurse). But to most of the inhabitants of Albert Square they're 'outsiders' – posh, even. Lou says Debs is too bossy by half – really 'stuck up'. Andy makes excuses for her.

Families and family life play a large part in everyday happenings in Albert Suare. Who's doing what, to whom and where is the constant chat of the neighbourhood. Gossip, intrigue and scandal are high on the list of daily events. Ask anyone . . . .

TONY HOLLAND

## The press

### Newspaper format

National daily and Sunday newspapers are often divided between 'quality' broadsheet and 'popular' tabloid. One obvious difference is the size. Broadsheets are twice the size of tabloid newspapers. This is one of the aspects of newspaper **format** – the size, shape, and content of the publication.

There are differences within broadsheet and tabloid formats. Some tabloids, like the *Daily Mail* and the *Daily Express*, occupy a midway position between broadsheets, like *The Times* and the *Independent*, and the 'pop' tabloids, the *Sun, Daily Mirror* and *Daily Star*.

***Figure 5.4***

### Activity

Compare the format of a national broadsheet newspaper to that of a popular tabloid. (You could start with the examples shown on pages 16–17.) Comment on the following aspects:

1. *Design*
   a. Size of print and photographs.
   b. Number of stories per page.
   c. The layout of stories and photographs.
   d. General graphics like print (e.g. use of italics or bold print), boxes, underlining of captions, quotes, etc.
2. *Content*
   How many pages and columns are devoted to:
   a. News – how much is British or foreign news? Which stories are covered? Are there news features?
   b. Entertainment and arts coverage.
   c. Other features such as finance and business, sport (which sports?), letters, astrology, crossword competitions.

### Magazines

Magazine formats vary much more than newspapers. Women's magazines are the biggest sector (see page 106 for a list of the top 100 magazines). The major high street newsagents subdivide the main categories or genres, so buyers can easily find most titles in their respective category.

### Activity

Select two examples of magazines or comics aimed at either children or teenagers. Examine the format of each with respect to:

1. Design – print, photographs, layout etc.
2. Categories of content.

## Pop music genre

From this sample of new album releases in one week there are at least 20 categories of music. Pop/rock and middle of the road (MOR) appeal to broad mainstream music styles, which dominate the singles and LP charts. As with all genres individual categories overlap, e.g. dance and disco or soul, and rockabilly and rock 'n' roll. It is certainly unlikely that audiences will apply the same labels to music as are used in the industry. What then makes a music genre?

| Artist Title Label LP No/Cassette No Dealer Price (Distributor) | Music Category |
|---|---|
| A POPULAR HISTORY OF SIGNS TASTE Jungle FREUD 17/— £3.65 (I/J) | Pop |
| ABSHIRE, Nathan PINE GROVE BLUES Ace CHD 217/— £3.95 (P) | Blues |
| ARRINGTON, Steve JAM PACKED Manhattan/EMI MTL 1015/TC-MTL 1015 (E) | Soul |
| BATHERS, The UNUSUAL PLACES TO DIE Go! Discs AGOLP 10/ZGOLP 10 (C) | Intellectual Pop |
| BELIS FROND MIASMA Woronzow W 003/— £3.65 (I/BK) | Psychedelic |
| BENATAR, Pat BEST SHOTS Chrysalis PATV 1/ZPATV 1 (C) | Rock |
| BIM SKALA BIM BOSTON BLUEBEAT SKA SKAR 002/— £3.05 (I/RE) | SKA |
| BREATHLESS THREE TIMES AND WAVING Tenor Vossa BREATHLP 6/BREATHCAS 6 (I/NM) | Rock |
| BURGESS, Sonny THE FLOOD TAPES 1959-62 Sunjay SJLP 561/— £3.69 (A/CSA) | Rock & Roll |
| CALZADO, Rudy RICA CHARANGA Globe Style ORB 025/— £3.45 (P) | Ethnic |
| CARRACK, Paul ONE GOOD REASON Chrysalis CDL 1578/ZCDC 1578 (C) | MOR |
| CLANNAD SIRIUS RCA PL 71513/PK 71513 (BMG) | Folk/Rock |
| COCOA TEA COCOA TEA Jim Peys JWH 871/— £3.79 (I/J) | Reggae |
| COGAN, Alma A CELEBRATION EMI EM 1280/— (E) | MOR |
| COLE, Lloyd & The Commotions MAINSTREAM Polydor LCLP 3/LCMC 3 £3.95 (F) | Rock |
| FLORIDA SUN FLORIDA SUN ALBUM Tembo TMB 117/TMBC 117 (IMS) | Pop |
| FORCEFIELD FORCEFIELD President PTLS 1088/PTLC 1088 (PR/SP) | Rock |
| FRACTURED NO PEACE FOR THE WICKED I.D. NOSE 17/— £3.05 (I/RE) | Rockabilly |
| FRANK CHICKENS GET CHICKENIZED Flying Lecords STIR 1/— £3.65 (I/RE) | Anglo/Jap |
| *FRANCIS, Connie GREATEST HITS Polydor (Germany) 8319941/8319944 £2.45 (IMS) | Pop |
| FROGGITS, The START FROM SCRATCH Tembo TMB 114/TMBC 114 (IMS) | Jazz |
| FURLONG, Michael BREAKAWAY Music For Nations MFN 79/— (P) | Metal |
| *GOYA, Francis THIS IS FRANCIS GOYA PolyGram (Holland) 8308281/8308284 £3.87 (IMS) | MOR |
| GRAHAM'S AFRO-CUBISTS, Kenny The CARIBBEAN SUITE/AFRO KADABRA Esquire ESQ 329/— (CA/H/I/IRS/SW) | Jazz |
| HAGGARD, Merle SINGS COUNTRY EMI EMS 1253/TC-EMS 1253 (E) | Country & Western |
| HARRIOTT, Joe with the TONY KINSEY TRIO JUMP FOR ME Esquire ESQ 326/— CA/H/I/IRS/SW) | Jazz |
| HAWKWIND THE OFFICIAL PICTURE LOGBOOK Flickknife/Spartan HW BOX 1/— (Limited Edition 2,000) £11.15 (SP) | Heavy Rock |
| HAYES, Isaac HOT BUTTERED SOUL Stax SXE 005/— £2.99 (E) | Soul |
| HEERA DIAMONDS FROM HEERA Arisma ARI 1004/ARI 0104 £3.05 (I/BK) | Asian |
| *HESSION, Carl ECHOES OF IRELAND Raglan (Ireland) RGLP 3/RGMC 3 £3.45 (IMS) | Irish |
| HURRAH! WAY AHEAD Efurient PACE 2/— £3.05 (I/RE) | Rock |
| JACKSON, Chuck A POWERFUL SOUL Kent KENT 073/— £3.45 (P) | Soul |
| JONES, George BLUE MOON OF KENTUCKY EMI EMS 1251/TC-EMS 1251 (E) | Country & Western |
| KALAPREET SHAVA SHAVA Arishma ARI 1003/ARI 0103 £3.05 (I/BK) | Asian |
| KREATOR TERRIBLE CERTAINTY Noise UK NOISE 086/— £3.85 (I/RE) | Trash Metal |
| *LAST, James MYSTIQUE Polydor (Canada) 2372162/3151162 £5.25 (IMS) | MOR |
| MAHLATHINI THE LION OF SOWETO Earthworks/Virgin EWV 4/TCEWV 4 (E) | African |
| MARRS, Johnny BORN UNDER A BAD SIGN Genie GENIE LP 2/LC 2 £3.05 (SP) | R & B |
| MEAT LOAF LIVE Arista 208 599/408 599 (BMG) | Rock |
| MINDREADERS, The BAN THE MINDREADER Empire SKILL 1/— £3.65 (I/BK) | Rock |
| *MOUSKOURI, Nana LOVE ME TENDER Philips (Canada) 8320391/8320394 £5.25 (IMS) | MOR |
| NELSON, Willie COUNTRY WILLIE EMI EMS 1252/TC-EMS 1252 (E) | Country & Western |
| NICHOLS, Grace and Samuel Selvon CONTEMPORARY LITERATURE READINGS National Sound Archive NSA C4 (cassette only) (British Library — 0937 843434) | Literature |
| *ORIGINAL SOUNDTRACK JEAN DE FLORETTE SPI Milan (France) A 235/C 235 £3.87 (IMS) | Film |
| ORIGINAL SOUNDTRACK TEEN WOLF Silva Screen SCRS 1010/— £3.75 (A) | Soundtrack |
| ORIGINAL SOUNDTRACK HEARTS OF FIRE CBS 460001/460004 (C) | Soundtrack |
| PARSONS PROJECT, Alan EYE IN THE SKY Arista ARISTA 258 718 (BMG) | Rock |
| PEPSI & SHIRLIE ALL RIGHT NOW Polydor POLH 38/POLHC 38 £3.95 (F) | Pop |
| PHENOMENA 2 DREAM RUNNER Arista 208 697/— (BMG) | Rock |
| PINK FAIRIES KILL 'EM AND EAT 'EM Demon FIEND 105/— £3.65 (P) | Rock |
| POOVEY, Groovey Joe THE TWO SIDES Sunjay SJLP 562/— £3.69 (A/CSA) | Rock & Roll |
| PRETENDERS THE SINGLES WEA WX135/WX135C (W) | Rock |
| PUKWANA, Cudu IN THE TOWNSHIP Earthworks/Virgin EWV 5/TCEWV 5 (E) | African |
| RICHARD, Little EARLY STUDIO OUTTAKES Sunjay SJLP 565/— £3.69 (A/CSA) | Rock & Roll |
| ROGER UNLIMITED Reprise K9254961/K9254964 (W) | Dance/Disco |
| RUEFREX PLAYING CARDS WITH DEAD MEN Flickknife/Spartan BLUNT 041/— £3.05 (SP) | Rock |
| SANTAMARIA, Mongo MONGO'S GROOVE B.G.P. BGPC 1001/— £3.45 (A) | Jazz |
| SCOTT, Ronnie AND HIS ORCHESTRA LIVE AT THE JAZZ CLUB Esquire ESQ 328/— (CA/H/I/IRS/SW) | Jazz |
| SCREAMING BLUE MESSIAHS, The BIKINI RED WEA WX117/WX117C (W) | Rock |
| SHAKA, Jah & The Mad Professor JAH SHAKA MEETS THE MAD PROFESSOR AT ARIWA SOUNDS Ariwa SALP 84/— £3.65 | Ska |
| SHINE, Brendan AT HOME Play PLAY 1020/CPLAY 1020 £3.65 (SP) | Irish MOR |
| SIDIKI DIABATE & ENSEMBLE BA TOGOMO National Sound Archive FMS/NSA 001 £4.99 (British Library — 0937 843434) | Ethnic |
| SINATRA, Frank SINATRA (1939-55) — THE RADIO YEARS Meteor MTBS 001/— (Box Set) (A) | MOR |
| STEWART, Mark MARK STEWART Mute STUMM 43/— £3.89 (SP) | New Wave |
| SYLVIAN, David SECRETS OF THE BEEHIVE Virgin V2471/TCV 2471 (E) | Rock |
| TAYLOR, Little Johnny PART TIME LOVE Ace CH 229/— £3.45 (P) | R&B |
| THESE IMMORTAL SOULS GET LOST (DON'T LIE) Mute STUMM 48/— £3.89 (SP) | New Wave |
| TJADER, Cal CAL'S PALS B.G.P. BGP 1003/BGPC 1003 £3.45 (A) | Jazz |
| TRIFFIDS, The CALENTURE Island ILPS 9885/ICT 9885 £3.75 (F) | Rock |
| 2AM WHEN EVERY SECOND COUNTS RCA PL 71400/PK 71400 (BMG) | Rock |
| VARIOUS ANTHEMS 4 Streetsounds MUSIC 12/ZCMUS 12 £3.79 (A) | Dance/Disco |
| VARIOUS BHANGRA FEVER Arishma ARI 1005/ARI 0105 £3.05 (I/BK) | Asian |
| VARIOUS BRITISH BIRD SONGS AND CALLS (2-cassette) National Sound Archive NSA C5/6 (cassette only) (British Library — 0937 843434) | Wildlife Sounds |
| *VARIOUS CASABLANCA DANCE HITS Casablanca (USA) 8840531/8840534 £3.45 (IMS) | Dance |
| VARIOUS DO IT FLUID: 6 RARE GROOVES B.G.P. BGPC 1002/— £3.45 (A) | Dance/Disco |
| VARIOUS FOCUS ON FUSION B.G.P. BGP 1004/BGPC 1004 £3.45 (A) | Jazz/Fusion |
| VARIOUS HEARTBEAT ZOUCOUS Earthworks/Virgin EWV 3/TCEWV 3 (E) | African |
| VARIOUS HURRICAN ZOUK Earthworks EWV 2/TCEWV 2 (E) | African |
| VARIOUS I LOVE MY CAR Fury F3002/— £3.50 (Fury — 0582 452258) | Rockabilly |
| VARIOUS JACKMASTER VOL 1 DJ International/Westside JACKLP 501/ZCJACK 501 £3.79 (A) | House |
| VARIOUS JAZZ JUICE 6 Streetsounds SOUND 9/ZCSND 9 £3.79 (A) | Jazz |
| VARIOUS LIVE AT JONG LEURS Spartan JONG 1/JONG C1 (SP) | Comedy |
| VARIOUS MEMPHIS ROCKABILLY Sunjay SJLP 568/— £3.69 (A/CSA) | Rockabilly |
| *VARIOUS MERCURY DANCE CLASSICS Mercury (USA) 8840011/8840014 £3.45 (IMS) | Dance |
| VARIOUS MUSIC OF THE TUKANO AND CUNA PEOPLES OF COLOMBIA Rogue FMS/NSA 002 £4.99 (British Library — 0937 843434) | Ethnic |
| VARIOUS STREETSOUNDS 87-3 Streetsounds STSND 873/ZCSTS 873 £3.79 (A) | Dance/Disco |
| VARIOUS THE PEBBLES BOX UBIK BOXX 1/— £16.50 (I/BK) | 60's Psychedelic |
| VARIOUS THUNDER BEFORE DAWN Earthworks/Virgin EWV 1/TCEWV 1 (E) | African |
| VOW WOW V Arista 208 678/408 678 (BMG) | Rock |
| WINWOOD, Steve CHRONICLES Island SSW 1/SSWC 1 £3.95 (F) | Rock |
| WRAY, Link GROWLING GUITAR Big Beat WIK 65/— £3.45 (P) | R&B |

### COMPACT DISCS

| | |
|---|---|
| ARRINGTON, Steve JAM PACKED Manhattan/EMI CDP 746903 (E) | Soul |
| BENATAR, Pat BEST SHOTS Chrysalis CCD 1538 (C) | Rock |
| CARRACK, Paul ONE GOOD REASON Chrysalis CCD 1578 (C) | MOR |
| CLANNAD SIRIUS RCA PD 71513 (BMG) | Folk/Rock |
| COLE, Lloyd & The Commotions MAINSTREAM Polydor 833 691-2 £7.29 (F) | Rock |
| *FLORIDA SUN FLORIDA SUN ALBUM Tembo TMBCD 117 £7.49 (IMS) | Pop |
| FORCEFIELD FORCEFIELD President PCOM 1088 (PR/SP) | Rock |
| FRANK CHICKENS GET CHICKIZED Flying Lecords STIR D1 £6.49 (I/RE) | Anglo/Jap |
| *FROGGITS, The START FROM SCRATCH Tembo TMBCD 114 £7.49 (IMS) | Jazz |
| KING, Albert THE BEST OF ALBERT KING — "I'LL PLAY THE BLUES FOR YOU" Stax CDSX 007 £7.29 (P) | Blues |
| MEAT LOAF LIVE ARISTA 258 599 (BMG) | Rock |
| MINIMAL COMPACT THE FIGURE ONE CUTS Crammed CRAM 055CD £7.99 (I/NM) | Rock |
| ORIGINAL SOUNDTRACK GHOSTBUSTERS Arista 610 238 (BMG) | Soundtrack |
| ORIGINAL SOUNDTRACK HEARTS OF FIRE CBS 460004 (C) | Soundtrack |
| PARSONS PROJECT, Alan EYE IN THE SKY Arista ARISTA 258 718 (BMG) | Rock |
| PEPSI & SHIRLIE ALL RIGHT NOW Polydor 833 724-2 £7.29 (F) | Pop |
| PRETENDERS THE SINGLES WEA WX 2422292 (W) | Rock |
| SHINE, Brendan COLLECTION Play CD PLAY 1 £7.29 (SP) | Irish MOR |
| SHINE, Brendan MEMORIES Play CD PLAY 3 £7.29 (SP) | Irish MOR |
| STEWART, Mark MARK STEWART Mute CD STUMM 43 (SP) | New Wave |
| THESE IMMORTAL SOULS GET LOST (DON'T LIE) Mute CD STUMM 48 07 05 (SP) | New Wave |
| TRIFFIDS, The CALENTURE Island CID 9885 £7.29 (F) | Rock |
| 2AM WHEN VERY SECOND COUNTS RCA PD 71400 (BMG) | Rock |
| VARIOUS ANTHEMS 4 Streetsounds CDMUS 12 £7.29 (A) | Soul Funk |
| VARIOUS JACKMASTER VOL 1 DJ International/Westside JACK 501 CD £7.29 (A) | House |
| VARIOUS JAZZ JUICE 6 Streetsounds CDSND 9 £7.29 (A) | Jazz |
| VARIOUS LOUISIANA CAJUN MUSIC SPECIAL Ace CDCH 914 £7.29 (P) | Cajun |
| VARIOUS STREETSOUNDS 87-3 Streetsounds CDSTS 873 £7.29 (A) | Dance/Disco |
| VOW WOW V Arista 258 678 (BMG) | Rock |
| WARWICK, Dionne HEARTBREAKER Arista ARISTA 258 719 (BMG) | Soul |
| WINWOOD, Steve CHRONICLES Island SSWCD 1 £7.29 (F) | Rock |

* Import

| | | | |
|---|---|---|---|
| Mon 26 October-Fri 30 October 1987 | Album Releases: 91 | Compact Discs: 31 | |
| Year to Date (43 weeks to 30 October) | Album Releases: 3,754 | Compact Discs: 1,611 | |

**Figure 5.5** (*Music Week*, 24 Oct. 1987)

**1.** *Sound*

The obvious ingredient is the sound – the choice of instruments, the singing style and possibly the lyrics.

**2.** *Style*

Apart from the visual style, there is the style of the performers and the audience. These include clothes, hair, accessories – the overall *look* which is associated with the music.

**3.** *Meaning*

The meanings created by differing musical sounds and styles depending on the surrounding culture. Pop music has always been linked to youth culture. Much of the pleasure of rock and roll in the 1950s was

# PUBLIC ENEMY

Chuck D. and Griff of Public Enemy tell Chris Heath about their hit single "Rebel Without A Pause" and explain why they're "deadly serious" about everything they do. . .

## REBEL WITHOUT A PAUSE

Jesse Jackson: Brothers and sisters brothers and sisters
I don't know what this world is coming to

Chuck D: Yes the rhythm the rebel
Without a pause I'm lowering my level
The hard rhymer where you never been I'm in
You want stylin you know it's time again
D the enemy tellin you to hear it
They praised the music
This time they play the lyrics
Some say no to the album the show
Bum rush the sound I made a year ago
I guess you know you guess I'm just a radical
Not a sabbatical yes to make it critical
The only party your body should be partying to
Panther Power on the hour from the rebel to you

Flavour Flave: Oh yo Chuck man I don't understand this man
Yo you got this one out man you're losing them

Chuck D: Radio suckers never play me
On the mix they just OK me
Now known and grown
When they're clocking my zone it's known
Snakin and takin everything that a brother owns
(Hard) my calling card
Recorded and ordered supporter of Chesimard
Loud and proud kickin live next to poet supreme
Loop a troop bazooka the scheme
Flavour a rebel in his own mind
Supporter of my rhyme
Designed to scatter a line of suckers
Who claim I do crime
They're on my time dig it

Flavour Flave: Yo Chuck I think we take the shorts
Sure this is cold medina man come on kick it

Chuck D: Terminator X Terminator X Terminator X
Terminate it

Flavour Flave: Yo Chuck you get them nervous
They can't handle this they're gonna break down

Chuck D: From a rebel it's final on black vinyl
Soul rock and roll comin like a rhino
Tabita turn suckers burn to learn
They can't dis-able the power of my label
Def Jam tells you who I am
The enemy's public they really give a damn
Strong Island where I got em wild an
That's the reason they're claimin that I'm violent
Never silent no dope gettin dumb nope
Claimin where we get our rhythm from
Number one we hit ya and we give ya some
No gun and still never on the run
You wanna be an S One Griff will tell you when
And then you'll come again
You'll know what time it is
Impeach the president pullin out my ray gun
Zap the next one I could be your Sho gun
Suckers don't last a minute
Soft and smooth I am I with it
Hardcore rawbone like a razor
I'm like a laser I just won't graze ya
Old enough to raise ya so this will faze ya
Playin the role I got soul too
Voice my opinion with volume
Smooth not what I am rough cause I'm a man
No matter what the name we're all the same
Pieces in one big chess game
(Yeah) the voice of power
Is in the house go take a shower boy
P E a group a crew not singular
We wear black Wranglers we're rap stranglers
You can't angle as I know you're listenin
I caught you pissin in your pants
You're scared of dissin us
The crowd is missin us we're on a mission y'all

Flavour Flave: Yo Chuck yo yeah man
You got em running scared man

Chuck D: Terminator X Terminator X Terminator X
Can the Terminator come on
Attitude when I'm on fire
Juice on the loose electric wire
Simple and plain give me the lane
I'll throw it down your throat like Berkeley
You see my car keys you'll never get these
They belong to the 98 posse
You want some more son you wanna get some
Bum rush the door of a store pick up the album
You know the rhythm the rhyme
Plus the beat is designed
So I enter your mind boys bring the noise my time
Step aside for the flex Terminator X

Flavour Flave: Yeah that's right
This jam is ready to cold medina boys
That's right cold medina
That's right you show nothing E F F E C T
Otherwise known as effect
You understand what I'm saying

***Source 5.6a*** Public Enemy

that it expressed a sense of rebellion and sexual excitement which appealed to teenagers (and upset adults, who sometimes tried to ban it).

Since the 1950s, different pop music genres have developed finding favour with a range of youth groups and cultures. These include mods and hippies in the 1960s and punk in the 1970s. Reggae music is one example with its roots in Afro Caribbean culture. The music is recognisable by its emphasis on a slow rythmic offbeat (provided by the bass). The music is also closely tied to the Rastafarian religion in both the lyrics and the performers' style (e.g. dreadlocks).

**Figure 5.6**

**Source 5.6**
Try and identify which genre of music is linked to each of the groups. Give reasons for your choice.

**Activity**

Choose one genre of pop music and describe:
1. Its distinctive musical sound, style and lyrics.
2. The typical singers/groups who produce the music.
3. Where and when the music is most often produced and consumed.

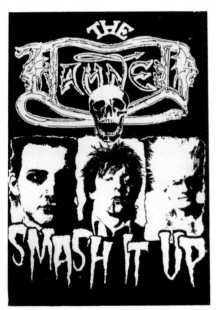

**Source 5.6b**  The Damned

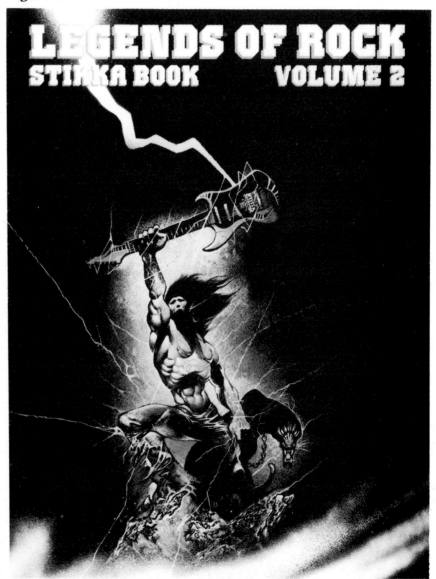

**Source 5.6c**  (Kerrang Spotlight, 3 Oct. 1987)

## Genre development

As said earlier in the chapter, genres rarely stay the same. One reason for this is audience need. A popular formula is unlikely to stay popular if it becomes too predictable. Also, new producers and writers will tend to add fresh ingredients by way of new situations, characters or even new technology as in science fiction.

Many of the themes of genres reflect wider social changes. For example, gangster films from the 1930s dealt with the activities of gangs involved in bootleg liquor during prohibition in the USA. The films were often based on actual gangsters' lives, such as Al Capone, or events like the St Valentine's Day Massacre. As America moved into the Depression of the 1930s, and social research began to reveal how crime was bred by urban deprivation, then there appeared a cycle of films looking at gangsters' social backgrounds and how they became gangsters. An example is *Angels with Dirty Faces*. Although in many post war Hollywood films it appeared as though organised crime was a thing of the past, by the early 1970s it was increasingly clear that in fact its influence was greater than ever. Films like *The Godfather* reflected the success and respectability achieved by the modern Mafia in America and Italy.

## Case Study: television police series

For the past 30 years, there have been a variety of police series on television.

*Source 5.7*
1. How have television police series changed since *Dixon of Dock Green?*
2. What do you think are the main ingredients of modern British television police series such as *The Bill?* Comment on: the leading characters (types, roles), the setting, the narrative (number of stories in each episode, whether any stories carry over to the next episode).
3. How do British police series compare with American series such as *Miami Vice?*

***Figure 5.7*** *The Bill*

### Dixon of Dock Green – a cluster of values

The character of George Dixon is never far removed from the centre of the action and his shadow is cast throughout the narrative.

Like the classic boy scout, Dixon was shown to be loyal, honest, trustworthy and brave. He was hard-working, dedicated, punctual, reliable, strong but never violent, forceful but not domineering, knowledgeable and helpful. The different facets of the character were developed in scenes with his superiors – whom he treated with due respect and humour; his colleagues – whom he worked with; younger policemen – whom he helped with care, concern and the benefit of his experience; the public – whom he worked for and who knew him as he knew them; and the villains – again people he knew and who came quietly submitting to Dixon's authority.

This vouches for Dixon's position as part of the community; not only does he work with them, but he lives amongst them. His experience is not that of a visiting policeman but of a member of the community; a neighbour and a friend.

***Source 5.7 a***

*The Sweeney* represents the pinnacle of the development of 'Action' in the British police series. The 'Action' series as they came to be known were heavily influenced by a stream of American films in the late 1960s which all featured a rogue cop as the central character – *Dirty Harry* (1971), *Magnum Force, Madigan* (1968), and *The New Centurions* – and the American television series which these influenced – *Kojak* (1973), *Starsky and Hutch* (1975), and other imitations too numerous to mention where the heroes were all on the borders of respectability. In these shows the concern for detail was overshadowed by the demand for action – movement, pace and violence synthesized with the sound track to produce the maximum effect. Many of the shows had greater flexibility in the camera work than the actors, with a constant search for new angles, new uses of slow motion and stop frame filming to heighten the action. Car chases had been around a long time – there is even one in the *The Blue Lamp*! – but in these shows they became obligatory, a very firmly established convention of the genre.

***Source 5.7 b***

### Drama on the streets of London

*The Bill* is different from other police series. There's a gritty realism about it. Shot on location in the East End, with a fine but-as-yet-almost entirely unknown cast, it is, says producer Michael Chapman, 'about the police being policemen rather than investigators in someone else's story'.

***Source 5.7c***   (*TV Times*)

***Source 5.7a/b***   (*Politics, Ideology and Popular Culture 2*, Open University, 1982)

# 6 AUDIENCE

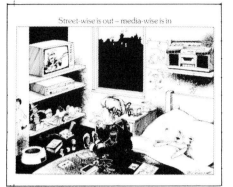

**Figure 6.1** (*Times Educational Supplement*, 3 Oct. 1986)

| Source: BARB | | Channel | Day | Time | Millions | TVR |
|---|---|---|---|---|---|---|
| 1 | (1) East Enders | BBC1 | Tu, Su | 19 30 | 22.8 | 44 |
| 2 | (2) East Enders | BBC1 | Th, Su | 14 00 | 20.0 | 39 |
| 3 | (3) Coronation Street | ITV | M | 19 30 | 16.3 | 32 |
| 4 | (5) Bread | BBC1 | Su | 20 35 | 15.8 | 31 |
| 5 | (4) Coronation Street | ITV | W | 19 30 | 15.7 | 31 |
| 6 | (7) 21 Years Of The Two Ronnies | BBC1 | F | 20 15 | 13.7 | 27 |
| 7 | (21) This Is Your Life | ITV | W | 19 00 | 13.4 | 26 |
| 8 | (6) Blind Date | ITV | Sa | 19 15 | 13.4 | 26 |
| 9 | (10) The Bill | ITV | M | 21 00 | 13.1 | 26 |
| 10 | (14) The Charmer | ITV | Su | 21 00 | 12.8 | 25 |
| 11 | (9) Boon | ITV | Tu | 21 00 | 12.5 | 24 |
| 12 | (17) Howard's Way | BBC1 | Su | 19 45 | 12.3 | 24 |
| 13 | (38) News, Sport, Weather | BBC1 | Sa | 21 15 | 12.0 | 23 |
| 14 | (51) Just Good Friends | BBC1 | Sa | 20 45 | 11.6 | 23 |
| 15 | (16) Whatever Next | BBC1 | M | 20 30 | 11.4 | 22 |
| 16 | (20) 3–2–1 | ITV | Sa | 17 45 | 11.4 | 22 |
| 17 | (13) Home To Roost | ITV | Sa | 20 00 | 11.3 | 22 |
| 18 | (18) Crossroads | ITV | M | 18 35 | 11.2 | 22 |
| 19 | (11) In Sickness And In Health | BBC1 | Th | 20 30 | 11.2 | 22 |
| 20 | (12) The Krypton Factor | ITV | M | 19 00 | 11.0 | 21 |
| 21 | (37) Play Your Cards Right | ITV | Su | 19 15 | 10.9 | 21 |
| 22 | (41) Live From The Palladium | ITV | Su | 19 45 | 10.8 | 21 |
| 23 | (19) Emmerdale Farm | ITV | Tu | 19 00 | 10.7 | 21 |
| 24 | (23) New Faces Of '87 | ITV | F | 19 00 | 10.7 | 21 |
| 25 | (22) Copy Cats | ITV | Sa | 18 45 | 10.5 | 21 |
| 26 | (27) Blankety Blank | BBC1 | F | 19 40 | 10.5 | 21 |
| 27 | (31) Crossroads | ITV | W | 18 35 | 10.4 | 20 |
| 28 | (24) Crossroads | ITV | Th | 18 35 | 10.4 | 20 |
| 29 | (15) Strike It Lucky | ITV | Th | 20 00 | 10.3 | 20 |
| 30 | (35) Bob's Full House | BBC1 | Sa | 18 45 | 10.2 | 20 |
| 31 | (28) Des O'Connor Tonight | ITV | W | 20 00 | 10.0 | 19 |
| 32 | (8) Bullseye | ITV | Su | 17 00 | 10.0 | 19 |
| 33 | (54) Highway | ITV | Su | 18 40 | 10.0 | 19 |
| 34 | (25) Emmerdale Farm | ITV | Th | 19 00 | 10.0 | 19 |
| 35 | (—) Name That Tune | ITV | M | 20 00 | 10.0 | 19 |
| 36 | (33) Telly Addicts | BBC1 | Sa | 17 45 | 10.0 | 19 |
| 37 | (44) Casualty | BBC1 | Sa | 19 55 | 9.9 | 19 |
| 38 | (30) News at 5.45 | ITV | M–F | 17 45 | 9.9 | 19 |
| 39 | (32) Ever Decreasing Circles | BBC1 | Su | 19 15 | 9.8 | 19 |
| 40 | (36) No Place Like Home | BBC1 | Tu | 19 00 | 9.7 | 19 |
| 41 | (—) Albert Hall Remembrance | BBC1 | Sa | 21 30 | 9.7 | 19 |
| 42 | (—) 'Allo 'Allo | BBC1 | Sa | 19 25 | 9.7 | 19 |
| 43 | (57) News And Weather | BBC1 | Su | 22 05 | 9.5 | 18 |
| 44 | (47) Last Of The Summer Wine | BBC1 | Tu | 20 00 | 9.3 | 18 |
| 45 | (29) Spitting Image | ITV | Su | 22 00 | 9.1 | 18 |
| 46 | (52) Benny Hill Show | ITV | Tu | 20 30 | 9.1 | 18 |
| 47 | (—) A Tribute To Eamonn Andrews | ITV | Th | 19 30 | 9.1 | 18 |
| 48 | (46) Brush Strokes | BBC1 | M | 20 00 | 9.0 | 17 |
| 49 | (39) Bergerac | BBC1 | W | 20 00 | 9.0 | 17 |
| 50 | (50) Dempsey And Makepeace | ITV | F | 21 00 | 8.7 | 17 |

Programmes with split networking may be under-represented

(*Broadcast*)

**Source 6.1** National top 50 (*Broadcast*, 8 Nov. 1987)

## Who is the audience?

### Audience size

The term mass media suggests large audiences. How large is revealed by surveys and sales figures regularly produced by media organisations.

1. *Television*

The Broadcasters' Audience Research Board (BARB) produces information concerning the numbers of viewers for individual programmes. It does it by issuing to a representative sample of viewers meters which record when their television is on, which channel and programme is being shown, and whether anyone is actually present in the room (by individual push buttons on a handset). These data provide the basis for the much publicised weekly **TV ratings** (TVR).

*Source 6.1* National top 50

1. Which programme types, or genres, appear to be the most popular?
2. Much has been made of the tendency of viewers to stay with one channel all evening, or for a programme which follows a very popular one to inherit its audience. Test this by drawing a line graph showing how BBC/ITV audiences go up or down during Saturday and Sunday evenings.
3. What effect might the growing use of video tapes for 'timeswitching' of programmes have on the validity of the ratings figures (or even on advertisers given the ability of video users to fast forward through adverts)?

## 2. Radio

There is no doubt that as television viewing has increased so time spent listening to the radio has decreased. The fact that the BBC uses interviews and Independent Local Radio (ILR) relies on diaries has led to very different figures being produced regarding which programmes are most popular. More difficulties are caused by ILR having few network shows (an exception being the Top 40 chart show), and the level of audience attention with radio listening is very uncertain (see pages 123–4).

## 3. Press/Magazines

Research by the National Readership Survey (NRS) concentrates on readership as well as circulation, reflecting the fact that single copies of newspapers and magazines may be read by several readers.

**Figure 6.2** (*The Listener*, 11 Dec. 1987)

| 1986 Radio audience share (%) | | | | |
|---|---|---|---|---|
| | Feb-Apr | Apr-Jun | Jul-Sep | Oct-Dec |
| IR | 27.9 | 27.3 | 27.8 | 28.7 |
| Radio 1 | 26.6 | 27.0 | 25.5 | 28.3 |
| 2 | 19.1 | 19.4 | 18.2 | 18.5 |
| 3 | 2.0 | 2.0 | 2.3 | 2.0 |
| 4 | 11.7 | 11.5 | 12.4 | 10.0 |
| Local BBC | 9.1 | 8.2 | 9.3 | 8.4 |
| Luxembourg | 0.3 | 0.5 | 0.4 | 0.5 |
| Other | 3.3 | 4.1 | 4.1 | 3.3 |

**Figure 6.3** (*Radio Audiences*, for Joint Industry Committee)

| All adult readership figures 1986 vs 1985 National dailies | | | |
|---|---|---|---|
| Publication | 1985 '000 | 1986 '000 | % diff. |
| The Sun | 11,706 | 11,396 | −2.6 |
| The Daily Mirror | 9,270 | 8,936 | −3.6 |
| Daily Mail | 4,854 | 4,721 | −2.7 |
| Daily Express | 4,973 | 4,509 | −9.3 |
| The Star | 4,222 | 4,271 | +1.2 |
| The Daily Telegraph | 2,903 | 2,852 | −1.8 |
| The Guardian | 1,513 | 1,460 | −3.5 |
| The Times | 1,381 | 1,249 | −9.5 |
| Today* | — | 1,088 | — |
| Financial Times | 733 | 736 | +0.4 |
| The Independent ** | — | 778 | — |
| | 41,555 | 41,996 | |
| | | (41,413) | *** |

*Mar-Dec 1986
**Oct-Dec 1986
***including proportional readership for Today/ Independent

| National Sundays | | | |
|---|---|---|---|
| New of the World | 13,022 | 12,756 | −2.0 |
| Sunday Mirror | 9,953 | 9,309 | −6.5 |
| The People | 8,932 | 8,372 | −6.3 |
| Sunday Express | 6,720 | 6,198 | −7.8 |
| The Mail on Sunday | 4,903 | 4,962 | +1.2 |
| The Sunday Times | 4,081 | 3,468 | −15.0 |
| The Observer | 2,377 | 2,352 | −1.0 |
| Sunday Telegraph | 2,409 | 2,250 | −6.6 |
| Sunday Today* | — | 781 | — |
| | 52,397 | 50,448 | |
| | | (50,315) | *** |

*Mar-Dec
**including proportional readership for Sunday Today

**Figure 6.4** (*Newspaper Readership*, Joint Industry Committee for National Readership Surveys)

**Source 6.2** Top 100 magazines

**Activity**

Produce a chart (pie or bar) illustrating the main areas of interest of magazine readers, e.g. women's magazines, music, motoring, etc. To reflect total numbers, you will need to make some rough calculations.

*the* **HOT 100**

**Source 6.2** (*Media Week*, 27 Mar. 1987)

| This year | Last year | Title | Publisher | Jan-Jun 86 | Jan-Jun 87 |
|---|---|---|---|---|---|
| 1 | 1 | RADIO TIMES | BBC | 3,064,530 | 3,044,679 |
| 2 | 2 | TV TIMES | ITP | 3,003,017 | 3,000,492 |
| 3 | 3 | READERS DIGEST | Readers Digest Association | 1,587,446 | 1,611,863 |
| 4 | 4 | WOMANS WEEKLY | IPC | 1,319,899 | 1,352,742 |
| 5 | 5 | WOMANS OWN | IPC | 1,055,286 | 1,113,080 |
| 6 | 6 | WOMAN | IPC | 1,021,242 | 1,061,967 |
| 7 | – | PRIMA | G&J UK | —— | 993,018 |
| 8 | 7 | WEEKLY NEWS | DC Thomson | 839,034 | 765,877 |
| 9 | 11 | WOMANS REALM | IPC | 613,710 | 625,469 |
| 10 | 9 | MY WEEKLY | DC Thomson | 642,131 | 607,065 |
| 11 | 12 | FAMILY CIRCLE | International Thomson | 583,416 | 598,202 |
| 12 | 10 | PEOPLE'S FRIEND | DC Thomson | 621,613 | 595,567 |
| 13 | 13 | WOMAN AND HOME | IPC | 541,515 | 587,909 |
| 14 | 8 | CHAT | ITP | 683,194 | 584,424 |
| 15 | 14 | SMASH HITS | Emap Metro | 517,360 | 512,317 |
| 16 | 15 | COSMOPOLITAN | National Magazine Co | 370,685 | 375,894 |
| 17 | 16 | GOOD HOUSEKEEPING | National Magazine Co | 335,436 | 345,321 |
| 18 | 18 | LIVING | International Thomson | 320,900 | 331,356 |
| 19 | 17 | FIESTA | Galaxy | 323,403 | 327,998 |
| 20 | 20 | ECONOMIST (WW) | Economist | 290,487 | 316,479 |
| 21 | 19 | MAYFAIR | Fisk | 312,962 | 279,280 |
| 22 | 24 | JUST SEVENTEEN | Emap Metro | 241,413 | 278,036 |
| 23 | 35 | IDEAL HOME | IPC | 196,414 | 242,471 |
| 24 | 22 | SLIMMING | Argus | 248,640 | 241,238 |
| 25 | 30 | ELLE | News International/Hachette | 217,342 | 239,605 |
| 26 | 29 | OPTIONS | Carlton | 218,210 | 236,117 |
| 27 | 21 | WEEKEND | Mail Newspapers | 281,769 | 231,366 |
| 28 | 27 | WOMANS JOURNAL | IPC | 227,686 | 230,320 |
| 29 | 23 | JACKIE | DC Thomson | 245,633 | 222,356 |
| 30 | 28 | EXCHANGE & MART (National) | Link House | 218,297 | N/A* |
| 31 | 25 | PRIVATE EYE | Pressdram | 239,887 | 216,021 |
| 32 | 33 | WOMANS WORLD | Carlton | 201,927 | 214,276 |
| 33 | 32 | SHE | National Magazine Co | 202,487 | 212,115 |
| 34 | 26 | LOOK IN | ITP | 236,858 | 208,838 |
| 35 | 31 | HAIR | Reed Business Publishing | 209,806 | 208,269 |
| 36 | 34 | HOME AND FREEZER DIGEST | BEAP | 200,619 | 204,083 |
| 37 | 36 | HOMES AND GARDENS | IPC | 192,826 | 198,188 |
| 38 | 38 | VOGUE | Condé Nast | 170,644 | 180,836 |
| 39 | 37 | COMPANY | National Magazine Co | 184,188 | 176,150 |
| 40 | 42 | SHOOT | IPC | 142,146 | 157,922 |
| 41 | 41 | KNAVE | Galaxy | 150,874 | 154,735 |
| 42 | 40 | ANNABEL | DC Thomson | 152,754 | 152,670 |
| 43 | 44 | TITBITS MONTHLY | Mail Newspapers | 137,651 | 148,009 |
| 44 | 39 | No 1 | IPC | 156,028 | 147,643 |
| 45 | 45 | LOOKS | Emap Metro | 137,017 | 147,430 |
| 46 | 47 | HOUSE AND GARDEN | Condé Nast | 130,395 | 137,022 |
| 47 | 56 | 19 | IPC | 110,012 | 136,660 |
| 48 | 61 | MIZZ | IPC | 104,531 | 133,959 |
| 49 | 46 | MOTOR CYCLE NEWS | Emap | 135,194 | 131,871 |
| 50 | 49 | CAR | FF Publishing | 125,705 | 129,262 |
| 51 | 54 | THE UNIVERSE | Universe Publications | 113,481 | 128,852 |
| 52 | 50 | RTE GUIDE | Eirann Publications Div | 125,552 | 127,201 |
| 53 | 48 | GARDEN NEWS | Emap | 129,716 | 125,477 |
| 54 | 51 | COUNTRY LIVING | National Magazine Co | 115,726 | 121,296 |
| 55 | 57 | HAIR & GOOD LOOKS | IPC | 109,318 | 121,141 |
| 56 | 69 | MOTHER AND BABY | Argus | 95,809 | 110,091 |
| 57 | 43 | BLUE JEANS | DC Thomson | 138,864 | 108,182 |
| 58 | 55 | ANGLING TIMES | Emap | 110,847 | 106,557 |
| 59 | 53 | GIRL | IPC | 113,991 | 105,285 |
| 60 | – | MY LITTLE PONY | London Editions | —— | 101,196 |
| 61 | 62 | PRACTICAL PHOTOGRAPHY | Emap | 103,064 | 101,116 |
| 62 | 58 | LIFE AND WORK | Dunfermline Press | 105,762 | 101,004 |
| 63 | 63 | TRANSFORMERS | Marvel Comics | 101,947 | 99,920 |
| 64 | 67 | COMPUTER & VIDEO GAMES | Emap | 97,876 | 99,530 |
| 65 | 52 | LOOK NOW | Carlton | 115,077 | 99,455 |
| 66 | 71 | HARPERS & QUEEN | National Magazine Co | 93,380 | 98,904 |
| 67 | 60 | NME | IPC | 104,648 | 87,733 |
| 68 | 59 | WEIGHT WATCHERS | GAT Publishing | 105,313 | 96,631 |
| 69 | 93 | CLASSIC & SPORTSCAR | Haymarket Publishing | 66,807 | 94,572 |
| 70 | 66 | SUCCESSFUL SLIMMING | Argus | 99,550 | 93,921 |
| 71 | 72 | PARENTS | Gemini | 91,500 | 93,500 |
| 72 | 65 | CRASH | Newsfield | 101,483 | 92,874 |
| 73 | 72 | FACE | Wagadon | 90,280 | 91,660 |
| 74 | 75 | PRACTICAL GARDENING | Emap | 84,825 | 90,382 |
| 75 | 75 | AMATEUR GARDENING | IPC | 84,503 | 90,368 |
| 76 | 80 | COUNTRY HOMES & INTERIORS | Carlton | 81,212 | 88,332 |
| 77 | 85 | OVER 21 | MS Publishing | 78,041 | 86,624 |
| 78 | 78 | TRUE STORY | Argus | 82,236 | 85,500 |
| 79 | 82 | GOLF WORLD | Golf World | 80,037 | 85,321 |
| 80 | 77 | NEW SCIENTIST | IPC | 83,696 | 84,543 |
| 81 | 70 | MY GUY | IPC | 93,894 | 82,975 |
| 82 | 84 | TRUE ROMANCES | Argus | 78,706 | 81,403 |
| 83 | 79 | SCOTS MAGAZINE | DC Thomson | 81,938 | 81,313 |
| 84 | 74 | SINCLAIR USER | Emap | 86,257 | 80,225 |
| 85 | 64 | CARE BEARS | Marvel Comics | 101,717 | 79,716 |
| 86 | 81 | COUNTRY MAN | The Countryman | 80,850 | 78,602 |
| 87 | 99 | ZZAP! 64 | Newsfield | 59,356 | 77,483 |
| 88 | 91 | TIME OUT | Time Out | 72,410 | 77,094 |
| 89 | 83 | MOTORING NEWS | News Publications | 79,659 | 76,431 |
| 90 | 86 | LOVING | IPC | 77,651 | 75,037 |
| 91 | 87 | GOLF MONTHLY | IPC | 74,471 | 75,021 |
| 92 | 90 | VOGUE PATTERNS | Condé Nast | 72,467 | 74,233 |
| 93 | 68 | PATCHES | DC Thomson | 97,010 | 74,102 |
| 94 | 89 | MOTHER | Argus | 73,029 | 74,005 |
| 95 | – | YOUR SINCLAIR | Sportscene | —— | 71,155 |
| 96 | 92 | IRISH FARMERS JOURNAL | Agricultural Trust | 72,240 | 71,055 |
| 97 | 88 | KERRANG! | Spotlight | 73,233 | 68,559 |
| 98 | – | MASTERS OF THE UNIVERSE | London Editions | —— | 65,254 |
| 99 | 95 | BIKE | Emap | 65,437 | 64,691 |
| 100 | 98 | WORLD OF INTERIORS | Pharos Publications | 60,789 | 63,641 |
| 100 | 96 | PUNCH | United Newspapers | 65,248 | 63,641 |

A ranking by Jan-Jun ABC figures for consumer magazines. Consumer magazines are defined as having a cover price, being sold through newsagents and listed in BRAD. We have excluded freely distributed magazines and those published through clubs and societies.
* Jan-Jun figure not available

**4.** *Cinema*

Compared to television, cinema viewing seems very small. In 1986–7 there was a slight upturn in admissions, weekly attendances averaging 1¾ million, following the steady decline since 1946 which is shown in the graph.

**5.** *Pop/Rock*

The graph (Figure 6.6) does not show the sales of compact discs, the most expensive music recordings, which had reached 8.4 million units by 1986.

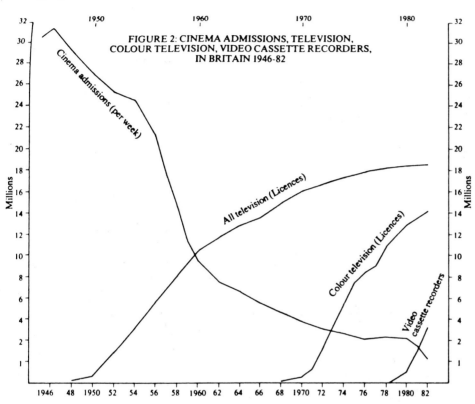

FIGURE 2: CINEMA ADMISSIONS, TELEVISION, COLOUR TELEVISION, VIDEO CASSETTE RECORDERS, IN BRITAIN 1946-82

***Figure 6.5*** (J. Tunstall, *The Media in Britain*, Constable, 1983)
(Cinema Admissions – Department of Trade; TV Licences – BBC; VCRs – Iain Muspratt)

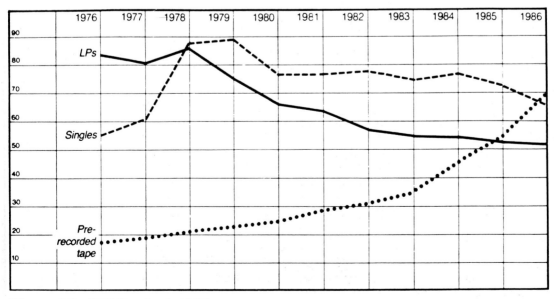

**Units. UK trade deliveries**    Millions of units

***Figure 6.6*** (*BPI Yearbook*, 1987)

## Daily patterns of media use

### Source 6.3

1. How might patterns of media usage differ at the weekend?
2. What seasonal variations may occur?

---

**Activities**

1. Produce a chart showing how attention to each media varies between 7.00 a.m. and midnight.
   NB: Tunstall's account predates breakfast/daytime/late night TV. How much they have altered the pattern could be determined by activity 2.
2. Ask a sample of people (representing differences in age, class and gender) to make a diary of their own daily media usage, which can then be compared to Tunstall's account.

---

*Jeremy Tunstall's account is based on various media audience surveys.*

Time of day or year greatly influences the kind of audience for radio. On weekdays, breakfast and driving-to-work give radio its peak audiences from 7 a.m. to 8.30 a.m.; the other early morning medium is newspapers. During the day there is a continuing lower level of use of newspapers and radio, both with housewives at home and with men and women at work. The mid-day meal break marks a small new blip in (morning) newspaper reading and in radio; it also marks the start of a significant audience for television. The afternoon sees a continuing decline in the radio audience, as television programming starts to attract audiences initially of housewives and retired people, but then of children returning from school.

In the early evening all the media battle it out together, not only with each other but with other activities such as preparing and eating food. At any time in the early evening fewer men are home, but of people already home a bigger proportion of men devote their prime attention to television. Around 6 p.m. many Britons are eating, the radio is beginning its final descent into an evening of negligible audiences, while the television audience is already large. Around 6 to 7 p.m. evening newspapers get their main readers, but morning newspapers are still being read. The majority of the evening television audience cue their viewing with a newspaper TV schedule. As the evening progresses some young people watch television and increasingly large proportions also give it their main attention. Television hits its peak audience around 9 p.m., and the 'truce' which ends at this hour is realistic in that fairly few children under ten years continue to view. The adult TV audience declines sharply after 10 p.m., and there is a small increase in the radio audience around 11 p.m. as people go to bed.

**Source 6.3**   (Jeremy Tunstall, *The Media in Britain,* Constable, 1983)

---

**Social class**

The means of identification used in advertising is 'social grade'. This is a classification based on the occupation of the head of the household, and it indicates the household's spending power. The table below shows the social grades, the occupation to which they refer, and the approximate proportions of each grade in the total UK population:

| | | |
|---|---|---|
| A | Higher managerial, administrative and professional | 3.1% |
| B | Intermediate managerial, administrative and professional | 13.4% |
| C1 | Supervisory or clerical and junior managerial, administrative and professional | 22.3% |
| C2 | Skilled manual | 31.2% |
| D | Semi-skilled and unskilled manual | 19.1% |
| E | Casual labourers, state pensioners and the unemployed | 10.9% |

*Figure 6.7*

# HIGH PROFILE

## THE VALUE

The Times has a higher percentage of ABC1 women aged 15–44* than any other quality daily newspaper.

Furthermore, The Times is the most cost effective quality daily newspaper for reaching ABC1 women aged under 45.

So if you're looking to raise your profile among young upmarket women, why pay more for less?

You simply can't afford to miss The Times off your schedule.

Telephone 01-833 7132 and ask for Jacquie Griffith-Jones.

## THE TIMES
quality at the right price

***Figure 6.8*** (*Campaign*, 10 Apr. 1987)

---

Children's favourite medium is television and those aged 5–15 are especially heavy viewers. Heaviest viewers of all are boys aged 15 or under – possibly because girls do more household chores. At 16 this changes radically. The 16+ age group are the lightest viewers of television – because they are often outside the home, or certainly the sitting room. They are the heaviest users of radio, records and cinema films. The 16+ age group are especially irregular *buyers* of papers; but they do read newspapers and buy magazines, often age specific ones.

Somewhere in the early 20s, and typically at the point of marriage, all this changes again. It is only at marriage – or setting up housekeeping – that Britons start both to buy and to read a daily paper; television viewing increases, and cinema attendance virtually ends – especially after the birth of the first child. People in their forties are typically quite heavy users for all the stay-at-home media: television, radio and newspapers.

People around the age of 60 are especially heavy readers of newspapers, but this drops off sharply after 65. Radio listening also declines. Elderly people are very reluctant to listen to Radio 1 and its contemporary sounds; many prefer the talk of Radio 4. Elderly people are also heavy television viewers (especially ITV). This heavy TV diet is a reversion back towards the youth pattern in another sense; while old people dislike youth culture and its music, they like children's television – substantial proportions of whose audience is old people viewing without a child present. Elderly people are great complainers about such things as excessive violence, explicit sex and lack of respect for authority; such attitudes probably partly explain their liking for children's programming.

***Source 6.4*** (Jeremy Tunstall, *The Media in Britain, Constable, 1983*)

---

## Social composition of audiences

This advert appeared in *Campaign*, a magazine for the advertising industry. It reflects the point that advertisers are usually intent on reaching or **targeting** a specific audience in terms of social composition. The three main factors are all included here: age, class and gender. Those with the most money to spend on advertised goods are 15–44, middle-class (ABC1 – see Figure 6.7) and female (women are responsible for about four-fifths of the purchases of domestic consumer goods) hence the greater number of media products aimed at such groups.

If advertisers can target the audiences most likely to buy their products, then they will avoid wasting money on audiences unlikely to purchase their goods, e.g. those who are too poor. An organisation which helps advertisers target audiences is the British Market Research Bureau. The BMRB surveys over 24,000 people each year, asking about their spending, lifestyle and media exposure in order to produce a **Target Group Index**. This can be used by advertisers to find out where best to place adverts. For example, BMW cars are not going to want to reach *Sun* readers, who are mainly working class and unable to afford such cars.

*Age and Class*

***Source 6.4*** Age and media use

---

**Activity**

Draw a graph or chart which shows how usage reflects different age groups.

---

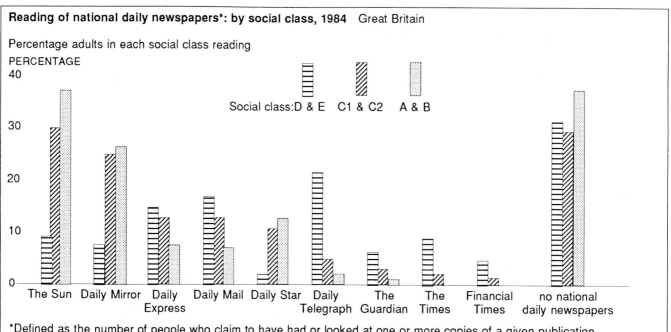

**Reading of national daily newspapers\*: by social class, 1984**   Great Britain

Percentage adults in each social class reading

Social class: D & E   C1 & C2   A & B

\*Defined as the number of people who claim to have had or looked at one or more copies of a given publication during a period equal to the interval at which the publication appears.

**Source 6.5**   (*National Readership Survey 1984*, Joint Industry Committee for National Readership Surveys)

*Source 6.5*

**Activity**

Try to identify the social class, and possibly age, of newspaper readers by examining the adverts in each paper (especially for jobs).

Although television is normally thought of as being very poor for targeting audiences (due to its large mixed audience), it is possible that with *Channel 4* advertisers might be able to pinpoint middle-class and younger viewers.

*Source 6.6*

Compare these programmes to those in the top 50 (source 6.1). How do they differ?

*Gender*

Although there are roughly equal numbers of men and women who watch TV and read newspapers, it is not surprising to find differences within each medium. Taking newspapers, men are more likely to prefer sport and politics, while women prefer features and entertainment. For magazines, there is a clear cut difference in the market.

**Top 20 programmes ranked by the proportion of upper middle class (AB) viewers**

**9 March – April 1987**

| Rank | Programmes | Ch | Day | Total no. viewers 000's |
|---|---|---|---|---|
| 1 | Horses | C4 | Sat | 453 |
| 2 | Horses | C4 | Sat | 400 |
| 3 | Keating | C4 | Wed | 324 |
| 4 | World at War | C4 | Sun | 429 |
| 5 | World at War | C4 | Sun | 333 |
| 6 | Plants For Free | C4 | Fri | 646 |
| 7 | Another Country | C4 | Thu | 509 |
| 8 | Rude Health | C4 | Mon | 496 |
| 9 | World at War | C4 | Sun | 418 |
| 10 | Cheers | C4 | Fri | 631 |
| 11 | News At Ten | ITV | Mon | 1299 |
| 11= | Intl Athletics | C4 | Fri | 534 |
| 11= | Fairly Secret Army | C4 | Fri | 340 |
| 14 | The Last Resort | C4 | Fri | 394 |
| 15 | Rude Health | C4 | Mon | 338 |
| 16 | The Last Resort | C4 | Fri | 533 |
| 16= | The Last Resort | C4 | Fri | 335 |
| 18 | 4 What It's Worth | C4 | Tue | 421 |
| 19 | Clive James on TV | ITV | Sun | 1997 |
| 20 | 1987/Film Performance | ITV | Mon | 859 |

**Source 6.6**   (*Media Week*, BARB, 1 May 1987)

1. Which magazine has **a.** the highest, **b.** the lowest proportion of middle-class readers (ABC 1)?
2. Which magazines are mainly read by young working-class girls?
3. Why is the bottom left-hand corner of the women's monthly periodicals table empty?

**Activity**

Try to place some of the newer titles of women's magazines on to the chart – such as *Mizz, Options, Prima* and *Just Seventeen.*

Men's magazines tend to be either sex magazines or professional and hobby magazines. Recently, attempts have been made to produce a male equivalent of the women's magazine with the emphasis on fashion and music. Examples include *Arena, the Face* and *Gentleman's Quarterly* (*GQ*). Indeed, it has been found that a considerable number of women's magazine readers are men (for what reason is not really clear).

**Source 6.8**  Gender, age and television viewing
On average, women watch for about 37 hours per week compared to 27 hours for men.
1. Why do you think there is this difference in viewing hours between men and women?
2. Try to explain the patterns of time spent viewing television in the table.

**Activity**

From a sample of males and females reflecting different age groups, conduct a survey to discover which programmes are most likely to be watched by each sex.

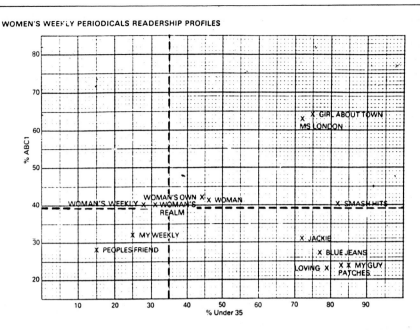

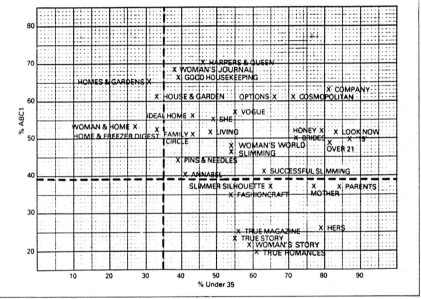

**Source 6.7**  Women's periodicals readership profiles, Women's weekly periodicals readership profiles, Women's monthly and bi-monthly periodicals, (*Media World Yearbook,* 1983)

**Average hours of viewing per week**

**Week ending 2 March 1986**

| Age | Total TV Hours Mins | | |
|---|---|---|---|
| Men | | Women | |
| 16–24 | 15 : 48 | 16–24 | 18 : 55 |
| 25–34 | 21 : 54 | 25–34 | 32 : 23 |
| 35–44 | 22 : 17 | 35–44 | 26 : 52 |
| 45–54 | 26 : 25 | 45–54 | 31 : 05 |
| 55–64 | 33 : 42 | 55–64 | 37 : 09 |
| 65+ | 39 : 00 | 65+ | 40 : 20 |

**Source 6.8**  (BARB/Channel 4, 1986)

## Minority audiences

Where production costs are low, and there is little dependence on advertising revenue, smaller 'minority' audiences may be catered for (as discussed in Chapter 3 with reference to radio, publishing and music). Popular music is a case where the audience has become increasingly fragmented, so that the top 20 singles or LPs no longer reflect the range of musical interest of audiences.

Source 6.9a

---

### Activity

Select one genre of popular music, e.g. reggae, heavy metal, etc. and try to find out the nature of the audience.

1. How large is it?
2. What is its social profile in terms of age, gender, class or ethnic origin?
3. How is the audience kept informed about the music if it is poorly represented on national radio and television, or in the best-selling music papers/magazines?

---

To answer these questions will require tracking down specialist music magazines, or finding an audience sample to interview.

*Gaps in the market*
From the commercial point of view, this means identifying audiences with purchasing power whose needs are not currently being satisfied. The launch of new newspapers and magazines is nearly always based on such gaps being recognised.

**Source 6.9**
Which 'new' audiences are identified in these two adverts for new titles?

Source 6.9b   (*News on Sunday in Campaign*, 10 Apr. 1987)

## Addressing the audience

Communication through the media rarely involves direct contact between the media producer and the audience (an exception being the radio phone-in.) How can those working in the media 'know' their audience in order to speak to them? Some feedback occurs through letters sent in, but it is doubtful whether these are really representative of the audience. Letter writers tend to be more middle class and educated. Surveys of audiences may be conducted, and ratings or circulation figures reflect general levels of popularity. Otherwise, those in the media must make do with an *image* of their audience, a 'typical' viewer, listener or reader.

### Audience position

As audiences, the media do address us, talk to us and weave us into the flow of communication. When we take a photograph or paint a picture we are providing a **point of view** for someone looking at the picture, as in this advert.

The same can be said of film and television, which have their own ways of positioning the audience.

Life isn't fair. Why is it that some people can achieve their ambitions, while others can't?

Take the cottage on the left. It may not be your cup of tea, but millions of people dream of retiring to somewhere like it.

Few will achieve their dreams. If you want to be one of them, how are you to go about it?

It's quite simple really. First, make sure you're 'with the Woolwich.'

On the happy day when the mortgage is finally paid off, you'll find yourself the owner of a valuable property.

If it was a Woolwich endowment mortgage, there would usually be an extra lump sum for you at the end of the term.

About now, if you've planned for them, all sorts of other nice things happen.

For example, the savings you've been making

## We'd like to lead you up the garden path.

Then you can begin to take advantage of all our different services.

As soon as you can, start putting money into a Woolwich savings account. (Have you checked our interest rates lately?)

The amounts you save aren't important. The great thing is to start early and keep at it. (It's astonishing how quickly money mounts up.)

When you have saved a deposit, you should set about buying your first house on a mortgage.

We can also help you with insurance services like our Homewise combined house and contents policy. If you want to furnish or equip the house, ask us for a Woolwich Multiloan.

all these years now amount to a considerable sum.

It's time to pick up the telephone and start ringing estate agents about rose covered cottages in the country.

Sounds easy, doesn't it? Well, it isn't.

When you're young, money is in short supply. Later, you will probably have the expense of a family. These days, continuity of employment can't be taken for granted.

But please don't give up.

If you pop in to any branch of the Woolwich and tell us about yourself and your dreams, we will do our best to help you make them come true.

**WOOLWICH**

ANYTHING'S POSSIBLE WITH THE WOOLWICH.

*Figure 6.9*

*Figure 6.10*

When telling a story, TV and film cameras usually construct a point of view. The camera shot creates the viewer's perspective on events. Generally, this is as an onlooker from the outside. The viewer then has the pleasure of knowing more than the characters in a story, since the camera will make sense of events for the viewer rather than the subjects. This can be the basis for suspense as we anticipate the outcome. For example, in the film *Psycho*, the camera switches between the 'victim to be', Janet Leigh, who is in the shower, and the approaching attacker with his knife. A more unusual point of view is provided in *Halloween* where the camera represents the view of the killer, so that the victim's look of shock is directed at us, the viewers. The camera's ability to position audiences like this helps to shape horror movies as a genre.

Audiences may also be positioned in terms of with whom they are led to identify. Through whose eyes are the events viewed? For example, in traditional westerns, the events are typically seen through the eyes of the 'hero' as opposed to the 'villain(s)'.

*Source 6.10* TV presenters
1. How do TV presenters help to position the audience for TV programmes?
2. Why are members of the public not allowed to directly look at the camera?
    An interesting exercise in breaking TV conventions, for those with access to video cameras, is to conduct an interview where the interviewee answers questions directly into the camera rather than the interviewer.
3. What effect does the auto-cue create for the presenter?
4. Apart from game and quiz shows, when else do presenters directly address the audience?

As explained in Chapter 1, such effects are **naturalised** through the various filming conventions, i.e. we are not made aware of how it is achieved, rather we simply take it for granted as audiences.

**Activity**

Video record a three minute sequence from a film shown on television, and write a short account explaining how the camera shots create a point of view.

This is rather different in non fiction television (as discussed in source 6.10 on TV presenters), where viewers are likely to be acknowledged verbally and visually (by direct address).

**TV Presenters**

Often, they appear to act as mediators, occupying a curious position half way between the sitting rooms of those watching and the experiences which are being shown on television. Their 'invitations' imply they can help us to enter otherwise obscure worlds. On documentaries they point out things we might miss; on talk shows, they introduce their famous guests to us.

This convention is exaggerated by the presenter's language, especially their use of an inclusive we. The presenter may say *'we* are going to talk to x': in reality they mean *they* are going to have the conversation while we eavesdrop. A similarly bizarre convention lies behind the tag lines of many presenters of light entertainment. It was all very well for Bruce Forsyth to proclaim 'Nice to see you; to see you nice' on *The Generation Game* but obviously he couldn't *see* the viewers at all. The same, of course, applies to all those hosts who sign off by saying 'see you next week'.

The most important device in this relationship, however, is that of *direct address*. Interviewees, especially ordinary members of the public are not usually shown looking directly at the camera. It is only presenters who can regularly 'catch the camera's eye' and stare at the viewers, a strategy which makes those watching feel they are being personally addressed.

The invention of the auto-cue – a machine which reflects the words printed on a roll of paper onto a mirror in front of the camera – helped to strengthen the ritual of direct address. Skilled use of this machine allows the presenter to speak continuously without looking down from the camera to consult notes. The smooth, fluent diction which results tends to give an intense impression of interest and knowledge, even if the presenter is simply parrotting words they don't understand.

*Source 6.10* (Jane Root, *Open the Box*, Comedia Methuen, 1986)

# Mode of address

Apart from positioning us as viewer, reader, etc., the media address us as people – that is they use ideas of who we are, and our relationship to the media as audiences. For example, newspapers use a language which is thought appropriate for its readers (see pages 16–17).

### Source 6.11

Describe how these front covers differ in their mode of address. Who are they addressing?

## Family and nation

The larger the audience, the more difficult it is to define its membership. Cinema's appeal has normally been one of privacy – the individual watching in darkness. In contrast, television (and previously radio) adopts a **domestic** mode of address – it is a family medium. Indeed, television family viewing policy provides four time bands for:

● Children.
● Family viewing or children alone.
● Children viewing with parents' approval.
● No programmes suitable for children.

Which kind of family is most often represented?
Families in Britain are more varied than in the past, e.g. one-parent families, childless families, families where the wife works and the husband is unemployed, etc.

Broadcasters, especially the BBC, have long addressed the audience in terms of a **national** 'family'.

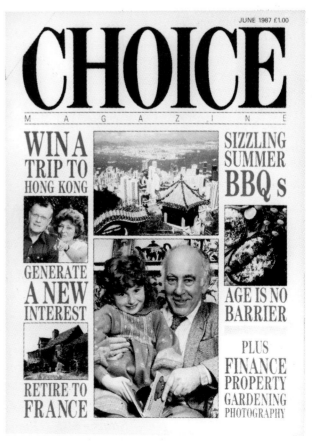

*Source 6.11*

## Source 6.12

These *Radio Times* covers reflect the prominence given by the BBC to what are seen as important national events. Indeed, the BBC sees itself as a national institution.

1. Which national events are represented on these front covers?
2. Why do you think the style of address has changed in these covers over the years?
3. Contrast the *Radio Times* with *TV Times* covers. Do they use differing modes of address? If so, why?

Nationality is also emphasised in an international context. TV commentators may distinguish between 'them' and 'us'. For example, in the Olympic Games or World Cup 'our team' or individuals' performances are highlighted to the exclusion of others.

> **Activity**
>
> Examine how national identity is created in the *Radio* and *TV Times* in previews of international sporting events or ceremonial occasions (particularly those involving the Royal Family).

**Source 6.12** (*Radio Times Diamond Jubilee* supplement, Sept. 1983)

*Source 6.13a*

*Source 6.13b*

## Gender

*Source 6.13*

1. How do these two adverts for jeans address different genders?
2. What do they say about masculinity and femininity?

In high street newsagents, there is usually a section of magazines for women. Apart from 'girlie' magazines, there is no equivalent section for men. This does not mean that magazines about cars, business, music, DIY, etc. are not addressing mainly male audiences. It is implied in the mode of address rather than made explicit.

How can these magazine covers be seen as addressing men?

---

**Activity**

Choose three examples of special interest or hobby magazines such as hi-fi, cars, angling, shooting, etc. Assess how far they seem to be addressing a male reader. Comment on the front covers, photographic style, graphics, colour, adverts, etc.

---

*Source 6.14*

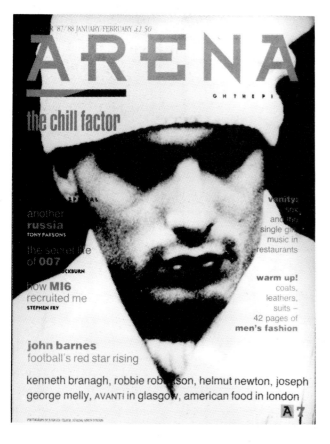

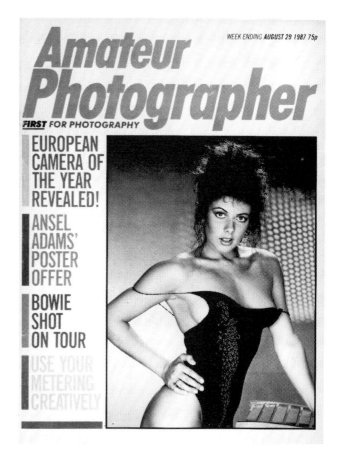

***Source 6.15***
Which kinds of women, in terms
of identity and lifestyle, are
addressed in these magazine
covers?

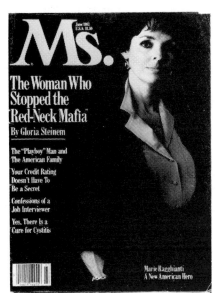

***Source 6.15a***

***Source 6.15b***

***Source 6.15c***

***Source 6.15d***

***Source 6.15e***

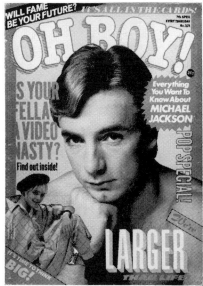

***Source 6.15f***

# How much influence?

Millions of people spend several hours of each week watching television, reading newspapers, etc. It is not surprising that many claims have been made about the media's influence on audiences.

## The passive audience

Throughout this century, it has been argued that the media have had a strong direct effect on audiences. Earlier in the century it was believed wartime propaganda and later Nazi propaganda in Germany were examples of this influence. In the 1950s, advertising was seen as persuading people to buy products in ways they did not realise. In these ways the power of the media has been likened to a **'hypodermic needle'**. Great concern has been voiced about the possible harmful effects of the media on young people. **Moral panics** have occurred in relation to cinema, radio, comics, pop music, television and most recently, videos.

*Source 6.16*  Video nasties What kind of effect on children do you think Mary Whitehouse is referring to in connection with watching videos?

## The media and violence: research problems

**1.** *The method*
Much of the research investigating whether violence in the media causes more violence involves setting up experiments, where young people are shown a diet of violent programmes, and then interviewed and/or observed to see how they have been affected. What might be the problems of this approach?

The essence of a video is that it is shown in the home and I'm afraid you know people who say that 'why shouldn't adults be able to see this kind of thing in their own home?' I'm half tempted to say that people who make that kind of demand knowing that children are likely to see it, aren't really themselves very mature and adult. There are places where people can go and see this material if they want it but we're talking about material in the home and there has now been tragic story after tragic story of the effect of this type of material on the children.

Mary Whitehouse (President, National Viewers' and Listeners' Association)

*Source 6.16*  (*Open Space*, BBC 2, 14 June 1984)

'I'VE TOLD YOU NOT TO WATCH THAT PROGRAMME! DON'T YOU KNOW IT CAN MAKE YOU VIOLENT?'

*Figure 6.11*  (*Daily Mail*)

## 2. Violence

### Source 6.17

How important is the context in which violence occurs? e.g. Who is committing the violence? How and why is it being committed? How does the violence relate to the genre of film, television programme, etc?

### Activity

Make a list of programmes whose content could be defined as violent. Try to rate them on a scale of 1–10 (10 being the most violent). Compare your ratings with the rest of the class.

### 3. What kind of effect?

Researchers cannot agree on how audiences are affected regarding violence. Among the effects suggested are:

a. **Imitation** meaning that some people will be encouraged to copy the type of behaviour shown (as suggested by the *Daily Mail* article in Figure 6.12).

b. **Cartharsis** meaning that by experiencing the violence second hand, audiences will be able to release their own aggression and frustration, and thereby become more relaxed and non-violent.

c. **Desensitisation** meaning that being exposed to a steady stream of violent images causes audiences to become numb and accepting rather than shocked or concerned.

The biggest criticism of the 'hypodermic needle' argument is that it does not fully take into account how active the audience is in receiving the media.

**Figure 6.12**   (*Daily Mail*, 21 Aug. 1987)

Dr. Belson in his much discussed 'effects' book, *Television Violence and the Adolescent Boy*, gives a classification of the 'Violence Rating' of a whole series of programmes. *Yogi Bear* gets a rating of 1.42, *Steptoe and Son* 2.39, *Hawaii Five-O* 7.25, and *The Great War* 7.62. Incredible as it may sound, they assumed that the BBC's series on the mass slaughter of the 1st World War affected audiences in the same way as a light-hearted cop series. According to Belson, both play a part in inciting teenagers to delinquency and both should be censored.

**Source 6.17**   (J. Root, *Open the Box,* Comedia/Methuen, 1986)

## The active audience

Doubts about how easily audiences are influenced by the media were raised by American researchers in the 1940s and 1950s. Their work showed that audience members used 'defence' mechanisms to resist media messages. These might include **selective exposure**, e.g. only reading a newspaper with whose political opinions you agree; and **selective perception**, interpreting what you see so that it is consistent with your current attitudes and beliefs.

Further 'protection' from the media was also found to come from the social groups to which audiences belong. As a result of this research, the original question, 'What does the media do to people?' was reversed to 'What do people do with the media?'

This question has been particularly pursued by semiologists (see pages 11–14), who see media products as texts which may be read (or **decoded**) in many different ways. The wider the range of possible meanings of any text, the more it is **polysemic**. Using the example of violence, it is doubtful whether audiences share the same interpretations of which films or television programmes could be seen as promoting or encouraging violence (consider the list of films mentioned in the *Daily Mail* article in Figure 6.12). As another example, look at the differing interpretations of Madonna in Chapter 1.

## Audience reception

What shapes our reception of the media?

### Uses and gratifications

This is based on the belief that audiences have certain needs (or uses) which they seek to satisfy (or gratify) in the media. The main four categories singled out are:

1. Diversion – escape or emotional release (forgetting everyday worries).
2. Personal relationships – companionship or for discussion (did you see . . .?).
3. Personal identity – making comparison with your own situation (do they have the same problem?).
4. Surveillance – seeking information about the world (what is going on?).

*Source 6.18* Radio uses and gratifications
1. Make a list of the uses and gratifications Crisell obtains from the different radio stations.
2. How far is radio different from other media in being able to supply so many needs in such a short space of time?
3. What other uses/gratifications might radio offer to audiences? To answer this, think of different groups of listeners and their needs, e.g. housewives, students, assembly line workers, etc.

*In this extract, Andrew Crisell describes how he hops radio channels in the morning on his way to work.*

Radio 1 starts the sequence because two of us are in the car and it is a better compromise of our tastes than any other network. Its output is lively and wakes us up. My daughter, being young, enjoys the music with a clear conscience and I, being less young, listen to it with an equally pleasurable sense of guilt. We are also impressed by Mike Read's imitations of all the other Radio 1 disc-jockeys. After I have dropped my daughter I feel less entitled to listen to Radio 1, and in any case stronger reasons call me to the nine o'clock news summary on Radio 4. First I wish to check my watch against the time-signal and secondly, although I have heard the eight o'clock news and scanned the headlines in the paper I was too sleepy to digest the former and the latter are already likely to be out of date. At five past nine I turn to Radio 3, having been made sufficiently wakeful by the sounds of Radio 1 and the catalogue of the day's crises on Radio 4 . . . Now, however, I feel the need to face work in a calmer, more thoughtful mood and *This Week's Composer* often helps to create this, especially if he is a favourite.

*Source 6.18* (Andrew Crisell, *Understanding Radio*, Methuen, 1986)

*Source 6.19* Researching uses and gratifications

This is part of a study of reasons for enjoying detective/crime series on television. Will you please indicate how strongly you agree or disagree with each of the following statements, by placing a tick in the appropriate column. (1 strongly agree, 2 agree, 3 neutral, 4 disagree, 5 strongly disagree.)

| Reason for watching | 1 | 2 | 3 | 4 | 5 |
|---|---|---|---|---|---|
| I like to identify with the hero | | | | | |
| I like to talk about the shows with others | | | | | |
| I like the tension of not knowing what is going to happen | | | | | |
| It makes me aware of how difficult a job the police have | | | | | |
| I like to imagine how I would cope with a violent situation | | | | | |

Etc.
*Note*
It is usually necessary to collect some data about the respondent: sex, age, occupation, educational level.

*Source 6.19* (John Fiske, *Introduction to Communication Studies*, Methuen, 1982)

## Levels of attention

The problem with the uses and gratification approach is that it assumes media usage is carefully selected by individual members of an audience.

Recent research into audiences suggests that peoples' attention to different media varies considerably. To reflect this, distinctions between primary, secondary and tertiary media activities have been made. Primary activity means giving the media close attention. Secondary activity means there may be other distractions such as talking to someone else, and tertiary means that the media is just in the background.

Obviously, these divisions are not precise, but it does recognise different levels of attention. Much depends on the medium in question. Compare watching a film in a cinema with listening to the radio whilst shopping in a supermarket!

## Source 6.20

1. Why do radio and television both seem to be secondary media in this survey?
2. Can you think of any circumstances when radio might become a primary medium for listeners?
3. How might being a secondary medium affect the way radio programmes are planned and presented?

It seems that television, too, is often a secondary medium. Indeed, in some homes, it is kept on continuously regardless of whether anyone is watching. This has been shown by the results of an interesting experiment when a small video camera was placed inside viewers' TV sets, so that they could be watched whilst watching TV! The extract (source 6.21) describes some of the findings of this experiment.

## Source 6.21  Television viewing in the home

1. Why might it be misleading to think of viewers as individuals?
2. What effects might remote control have on the way television is viewed at home?
3. Who do you think is likely to have most influence over the remote control and why?

This research also shows that whether someone is present or paying attention whilst a programme is on depends on the type of programme.

The evidence of the videotapes shows that people have their eyes on the screen only about 65 per cent of the time that they are in the room. For the rest of the time they attend to the kids, groom themselves, read the newspaper or doze off – the list of distractions is endless. The tapes also show that even when people have their eyes glued to the screen, they frequently engage in activities that have nothing to do with television-watching. A high proportion of these activities, like ironing, knitting, sewing and talking on the telephone while watching TV, are performed by women. This could be due to the sense of guilt that women report about watching television, but it may also be related to the fact that they have more domestic work to do.

One of the striking things to emerge from the tapes is the frequency with which people's viewing patterns are influenced by the choice and actions of others. Ever since media researchers first turned their attention to television, they have happily assumed that the best way to study television is to look at individual viewers – at the programmes they enjoy, how much they remember, and the effect that television has on them. Because television research has concentrated on the experiences of individuals, it has

*Source 6.21*  (Peter Collett, *The Listener,* 22 May 1986)

| Activities and Use of Radio and Television between 7.30 and 7.45 on Weekday Mornings, Summer, 1983 | | | |
|---|---|---|---|
| | Total % | Men % | Women % |
| Eating/drinking | 16 | 15 | 17 |
| Washing/dressing | 13 | 7 | 15 |
| Preparing food/ washing up | 10 | 6 | 18 |
| At work/school | 8 | 14 | 5 |
| Talking/phoning | 7 | 5 | 8 |
| Travelling to work/school | 7 | 7 | 3 |
| Housework | 6 | 3 | 12 |
| Care of children | 5 | 2 | 11 |
| Reading/writing | 4 | 5 | 3 |
| Care of pets | 2 | 1 | 2 |
| Hobbies & games | 1 | 1 | 0 |
| Gardening | 1 | 1 | 0 |
| Relaxing | 1 | 2 | 1 |
| Listening to radio | 23 | 21 | 29 |

*Source 6.20*  (Nadine Dyer, *BBC Audience Research Findings*, 1986)

overlooked the essentially social nature of a good deal of television watching. Even today, with the number of multi-set homes and VCRs growing, it remains the case that a fair amount of viewing takes place when more than one person is in the room. Under these circumstances, it frequently happens that family members want to watch different programmes, or that one person wants to watch television while another wants to do something that conflicts with TV viewing. The video material is full of such instances – cases, for example, where the man wants to watch *Match of the Day* and his wife wants to watch a feature film, or where the children want a bedtime story and the parents remain determined to watch the news.

Conflicts of interest over the television often lead to family disputes, to bouts of sulking and, more frequently than one imagines, to physical tussles over the remote control. The remote control has become the latest symbol of power. Parents will go to enormous lengths to withhold it from their children, and children will use all kinds of tricks to keep it away from their siblings. We have even recorded one case where the father gets up to make a cup of coffee for his wife and takes the remote control to the kitchen with him.

**Source 6.22**  Television presence and attention

### Activity

During two or three evenings in your home, or a friend's home, record in a diary:
1.  Who is present during each programme.
2.  How much attention is paid to the programme by each individual.
3.  The type of programme.
4.  Who decides the choice of programme.
Compare your results to the findings below.

Much of this research is still in its early stages. With respect to families at home, it seems that television might increase conflicts already present in some families or be used as a way of avoiding talking to each other. On the other hand, it might be a point of common discussion, bringing the family together, e.g. at mealtimes.

### Gender and reception

One aspect that the research has raised is how males and females differ in their reception of the media. One researcher, David Morley, has found that men are more likely to plan their television viewing in advance than women, e.g. checking the television listings. Furthermore, the men have a clear preference for viewing silently without interruption so as not to miss anything, whilst women tend to think of TV as a social activity, perhaps carrying on conversations whilst viewing. Another difference includes preferred programmes with male viewers opting more for sport and women for soap opera. Some of the reasons why this might be so are offered in the comments made to Dorothy Hobson (DH) in her interviews with female viewers of *Crossroads*, which is a soap opera (see source 6.23, page 126).

| Likelihood of full presence while programme on | Likelihood of full attention to programme while present |
|---|---|
| HIGH | |
| SOAP OPERAS & SERIALS | LIGHT ENTERTAINMENT |
| NEWS | FACTUAL PROGRAMMES |
| LIGHT ENTERTAINMENT | NEWS |
| ADVERTS | CRIME/ACTION SERIES |
| CRIME/ACTION SERIES | ADVERTS |
| FACTUAL PROGRAMMES | SOAP OPERAS & SERIALS |
| LOW | |

**Source 6.22**  (*Airwaves*, IBA, Spring 1987)

**Source 6.23** *Crossroads* and its audience

1. List the main reasons why *Crossroads* appeals to female viewers.
2. Why then do you think soap opera has more appeal for women than men?

As described in source 6.21, women are often unable to give full attention to the media because of domestic tasks like cleaning, cooking or child minding. Even so, there are occasions when women are able to watch television, read magazines, listen to the radio, etc. without distractions or resistance from others. This most typically occurs when they are at home during the day. Ann Gray reports that it is not unusual for groups of women to view hired videos, one popular form being the long family saga covering 2–3 tapes.

In drawing together the different types of film and television with different viewing contexts, she produced the table in source 6.24.

**Source 6.23** (Dorothy Hobson, *Crossroads, the Drama of a Soap Opera*, Methuen, 1982)

(DH = Dorothy Hobson, who is the interviewer in these discussions)

**DH** I wonder when men criticize it and say it's rubbish and all that. I mean, it occurs to me that if it was such rubbish then why do they make such a fuss about women watching it?

**J** They don't like it 'cos it's sometimes sentimental.

**DH** And you think women like it for that reason?

**J** Yes, because men are not supposed to show their emotions and feelings and so if they watch Crossroads and something comes on like Glenda and Kath talking, then they think it's just stupid and unrealistic because they are not brought up to accept emotional situations.

**DH** So you think it is more a programme that women like?

**J** Yes, it is, I think. I don't know any men who watch it.

**DH** I know some but certainly not many. But not only do they – I mean not watch it, but some of them are really quite hostile to their wives watching it.

**DH** Why do you like Crossroads?

**A** Just that you like to know what's going to happen next, you know. I mean they're terrible actors, I know that and I just see through that, you know. I just, now and then I think, 'Oh my God, that's silly,' you know, but it's not the acting I'm interested in, it's what's going on. I suppose I'm nosey . . .

**J** Well, it's easy to watch.

It's not relaxing but it's not something that's, like, tense. I mean, you follow the stories but you are not sort of keyed up about it. It's sort of tea-time viewing but not in the sense that you would usually use tea-time viewing, do you know what I mean?

**DH** What do you mean when you say, 'Not in the sense you would normally use tea-time viewing'? How would you normally use it then?

**J** Well people have got to stop and watch Crossroads 'cos it's on at teatime but with other things you are like rushing around getting the tea and talking and it's sort of in the background.

**DH** So you would never have it on in the background? You would always stop and watch it?

**J** No, you couldn't follow it.

**M** I like family stories and things like that. I like something with a story.

**DH** So do you think that's the reason that you like it?

**M** Yes, because it continues, and personally I think it's a lot like real life.

**DH** In what way?

**M** Well, I mean Jill had her ups and downs, didn't she, and so did Meg, and whatsit with her kiddie who she wants from America, I mean that can happen in real life, can't it. To me it's things in there that can happen in real life. It's not fiction to me. To me it's a real family story.

**Source 6.24**
For each of the four contexts, try to explain the choice of film and television programmes listed in the table.

| Types of viewing contexts | | |
|---|---|---|
| **Context** | **Film** | **TV** |
| 1 Family together | *Superman* <br> Walt Disney <br> *Jaws* <br> Comedy | Children's TV <br> Quiz shows <br> Comedy <br> *EastEnders* |
| 2 Male and female partners together | *An Officer and a Gentleman* <br> *Kramer v. Kramer* <br> The Rockys <br> Any Clint Eastwood | *Aufwiedersehen Pet* <br> *Minder* <br> Shows <br> *Coronation Street* <br> *EastEnders* |
| 3 Male alone | War <br> Action adventure* <br> Horror* <br> Adults* | Sport <br> News <br> Documentaries |
| 4 Female alone | *Who Will Love My Children?* <br> *Evergreen* <br> Romance | *Coronation Street* <br> *Crossroads* <br> *Dallas* <br> *Dynasty* <br> *A Woman of Substance* <br> *Princess Daisy* |
| *These are the category headings used by many video libraries | | |

**Source 6.24**   (H. Baehr, G. Dyer, *Boxed in: Women and Television*, Pandora, 1987)

# Audience access

The influence of the audience may be felt by whether people buy newspapers or watch television, etc. This, however, is only a crude reflection of audience reactions to what is produced. How far can viewers, listeners and readers directly communicate their feelings to media producers?

**Activity**

List as many ways as you can think of by which it is possible to contact television/radio broadcasters and newspaper/magazine publishers to give your views about what they produce.

Individuals may not be able to have much influence on their own. By joining an organised group, you may be taken more seriously. Apart from groups like political parties and trade unions, there are some organisations set up solely to influence the media.

**Source 6.25** Media pressure groups

1. What seems to be the aims of each of these organisation?
2. Who do you think has most power in the relationship between media producers and the audience? Give reasons for your answer.

**Source 6.25a**

# MEDIA MANIFESTO

CAMPAIGN FOR PRESS AND — BROADCASTING FREEDOM

## Can we tell them what we want or do they tell us what to think?

# The unacceptable face of the British media

## THE RIGHT TO COMMUNICATE

The razor wire around Rupert Murdoch's Wapping printworks is the symbol of press freedom in Thatcher's Britain — the freedom of proprietors to do what they want with their workforce, and determine what we should read.

Few people can now doubt what the "technological revolution" means when the media are in the hands of powerful magnates whose main concern is making money. It enslaves us all to their whims.

5,500 people lost their jobs with News International after years of service, because one man decided he could make more money that way and expand his international media empire. The police put an entire community under siege to ensure that Sun Bingo, and its sensationalised sex, violence and racism, reached the newsagents.

The rest of the media did little to sound the alarm bells for democracy.

In a scramble to win readers and advertisers, newspaper proprietors responded to the "unfair" advantage stolen by Eddie Shah and Murdoch's brutal tactics with mass redundancies and the introduction of "new" technology (which has been around for years) to reduce overheads.

All were prepared to form new companies and tear up existing agreements with the unions, who were cited as the real threat to press freedom as if printers have more power than proprietors, the courts or the government.

Meanwhile the government, intent on stripping us of public assets, had sold off an essential service — our main communications system, British Telecom.

The Home Office, which supposedly controls the airwaves on our behalf, is keen to see local broadcasting entirely in commercial hands. And if the government does sell off parts of the BBC, where 4,000 redundancies were announced last year, advertisers will soon have sole rights to determine what we hear on the radio and see on TV.

Rupert Murdoch, who has campaigned against the BBC's "monopoly" and its licence fee,

---

## OUR DEMANDS

★ THE RIGHT TO KNOW

★ THE RIGHT TO FAIR REPRESENTATION

★ ACCESS & ACCOUNTABILITY

★ WORKERS' PARTICIPATION

★ THE RIGHT TO MAKE CONTACT

★ FREEDOM OF THE AIRWAVES

★ FACILITIES FOR ALL

★ THE RIGHT OF REPLY

---

and Robert Maxwell who, like him, has extensive cable and satellite TV interests, and are among the most likely to profit from its break up.

Channel 4, set up with a brief to give airtime to "minority" interests, has abandoned its lofty ideals in the face of commercial pressure and may soon be cut adrift to fend for itself.

All these moves have frightening implications for democracy. If our sources of information are in the hands of multi-national media corporations who manage communication according to their own vested interests, we can expect to be treated simply as consumers with no rights.

Our daily dose of what the media tells us has convinced many that there are no alternatives. Yet more and more people are dissatisfied if not downright

angry at the way the media operate.

Media treatment of women, the peace movement, black people and trades unionists, lesbians and gay men, people with disabilities, or anyone who dissents from the free market notion of how society should be run, is a scandalous affront to our democratic rights. Small wonder that journalists are held in such low esteem.

The CPBF, backed by the trades union movement, believes that there are alternatives.

Our Media Manifesto highlights some of the main issues that should be debated publicly in the run up to the next election, and sets out legislative changes for press and broadcasting freedom in Britain.

---

The CPBF believes that EVERYONE should have the right to information, news and opinion, and the right of access to the printed word and to the airwaves, so long as such rights are not abused to incite violence, race hatred or sexual discrimination.

Those who control the media should be publicly accountable. News, information and communication systems should be considered a public service not a means of amassing huge private profits.

That means ending the media monopolies; introducing direct democratic control over the BBC and other broadcasting bodies; encouraging diversity and equal opportunities in all aspects of the media and at all levels; and making the media more accessible and responsive to the needs and interests of consumers.

Traditional notions of democracy have been profoundly changed by the present government. We need to reassert our democratic rights, and push forward our right to know, respond and participate.

In the run up to the next election the CPBF hopes to provoke public debate around the present crisis in the media.

Our Manifesto incorporates ideas raised in the four Royal Commissions on the Press since 1947 and a series of official Reports on Broadcasting, along with others developed by the Campaign since it was set up.

We shall be holding conferences and public meetings throughout the country to collect responses and challenge all political parties on their attitude towards the unacceptable face of the British media.

*Copies of the Manifesto are available to organisations willing to distribute it to their members.

*The CPBF is happy to provide speakers, and information to any organisation, that wants to challenge the power and privilege of the media and take forward the debate about what sort of media we deserve.

*We are keen to receive YOUR responses to this draft document, and what YOU think should appear in the final revised version. Fill in the tear off slip inside and send it to:

CPBF Media Manifesto,
9 Poland Street,
London W1 3DG

---

*Source 6.25b*

# PRACTICAL PROJECT WORK

Throughout this book there has been an emphasis on practical activities as a means of learning about and understanding the media. This approach is very much based on an ancient saying:

I hear and I forget;
I see and I remember;
I do and I understand.

The wisdom of this seems particularly applicable to an understanding of the media. We have seen that media texts are constructed, and that this process of construction is influenced not only by the available technology, but by a complicated series of codes and conventions, and by sets of production and audience expectations. What better way is there to understand this process than by producing a piece of practical work yourself?

Let's take photography as an example. Of course, looking at a photograph and analysing its composition, its use of lighting, and all the other codes it draws upon does lead to a greater understanding of how a photograph generates meaning, and this is an important process. However, actually using a camera yourself and trying to apply your understanding in a practical way leads to a first-hand appreciation of the ways in which a photographic text is constructed.

If we are right about the importance of practical work, then producing your own photographs should lead to a greater understanding of photographs taken by other people, just as analysing their photographs ought to help you produce 'better' photographs yourself. Theory and practice should inform and re-inforce each other and this will apply, not just

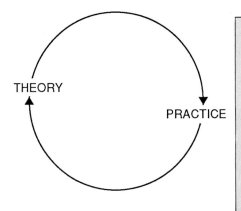

THEORY

PRACTICE

to photography, but to video and television, film, pop music and radio as well.

As we have seen, studying the media involves thinking about media

*FORMS and LANGUAGE*;

about the ways in which the media offer us

*REPRESENTATIONS*

of the world around us; about the

*INSTITUTIONS*

which own, control and therefore determine the types of programmes and media products we come across; and about the ways in which

*AUDIENCES*

use and make sense of the media.

It is important to think about these issues before you get down to producing your own practical work.

## Activity

Either individually, or as a small group, make a list of three ideas for a possible project you might like to do, e.g. a fanzine on a Heavy Metal group, a video about litter, a radio programme about life at school. How does what you know about media forms and language, representation, institutions and audiences relate to your three ideas?

## Warning!

Although practical work is a very important part of your media course, it is not one of the aims of the practical project to get you to try to copy or 'ape' the work of media professionals. Remember, they have much more time and money than you will have available, and they have access to a wide range of very sophisticated equipment which you will not have. Of course, you will want to make your finished product as good as possible, but the real point of practical work is to enable you to experience some of the processes involved in the construction of media texts, so that you understand in a critical way how and why the media work in the ways they do. In this sense, your ability to reflect upon and evaluate both the processes you go through and the finished product are every bit as important! It is because of this that you will need to keep a production log, not just to detail your personal contribution to the practical project, but as an opportunity to reflect critically and constructively about the experiences you are going through, and as a way of evaluating your finished product.

## Beginning the process

Although this chapter comes towards the end of the book, practical production work is something that you have been doing throughout your course. For example, in looking at the relationship between words and images on page 13, you will have experimented with writing new captions for magazine and newspaper pictures so that new meanings are constructed. During the introductory work on Madonna, you may well have designed a poster for a forthcoming Madonna tour of Britain. In this way, you will have already come across many of the issues which need thinking about when producing your main practical project. Before we look at the stages you need to go through, it is worth pointing out that the best projects are those that

> THINK SMALL
>
> and
>
> THINK REALISTICALLY

In other words, some of the best practical work comes from being aware of what it is possible to do well, within the time you've got, with the equipment you have, and with the other resources at your disposal.

## Individual or group work?

The first decision you must take is whether you want to produce a project on your own, or whether you would prefer to – and perhaps need to – work with other people in a group. It is quite possible to produce a booklet or a radio programme on your own, but it is worth remembering that the vast majority of media programmes and products we come across are produced by many people, often with specialist skills, co-operating and working together.

If you do decide to work as a member of a group, you will need to agree on who does what, to decide on individual and group tasks. For example, if your group is making a video, is one person only going to operate the camera, or are you going to let everyone have a go at doing all the tasks involved in your project?

## Choosing a subject and a medium

Your first task will be to decide upon your choice of subject and your choice of medium. Remember, choosing a subject involves not only what you want to say, but also the audience to whom you want to say it, in a way that is appropriate for that audience. You must also keep in mind what institutional limitations you will have to work with, such as the time available, how much help you might need from your teacher, the equipment and other resources available, the sort of locations you can realistically use, as well as the need to avoid a total disruption of the school or college! It is possible that you may have to reject some good ideas as being impractical, but you should use this as an opportunity to discuss why such an idea cannot be put into practice.

At the same time as you are choosing what to say and whom to say it to, you are probably developing some ideas as to how to say it; in other words, what medium you want to work with. Again, you need to think very carefully about this, for two basic reasons: firstly, there is no point in choosing, say, to work in video if your school or college simply doesn't have video equipment; secondly, you need to think very carefully about using an appropriate medium for your subject and its content.

Something that makes a good radio programme does not necessarily make a good video.

> **Activity**
>
> Once you have decided on a subject, discuss how this would be treated in each of the following media:
>
> Video Film Radio Print
>
> It will help you to write down your ideas on a sheet like that in Figure 7.1 or you might like to design your own sheet to suit your purposes.
>
> Which is the most appropriate medium for your subject?

## The stages of production

Before we go on to consider each medium in more detail, it is worth outlining the basic stages you will need to go through whichever medium you work with. Professional media production defines these basic stages as

> Pre-production
> Production
> Post-production

Although you will not be using the same sophisticated and expensive equipment as the professionals, it is useful to remind yourself of what is involved in each of these three stages.

**Pre-production** involves the processes of planning and preparation. This will include researching and gathering the information you will need for your project, as well as making contact with other people who will be of help to you in your project. You must also make advanced arrangements to use whatever facilities and locations you think you will need. There is no point, for example, in just turning up to your local library and expecting the librarian there to talk to you, be interviewed, or let you take photographs; you must make arrangements to do these and anything else you want to do well in advance! Pre-production also involves making detailed plans, designs, scripts and storyboards before you can go on to actually making your product or programme. Remember, all this work needs to be recorded and kept in your log-book or diary, together with comments as to why each element is important.

**Production** involves using equipment and other facilities to actually make your programme, magazine, exhibition or whatever it is you are working on. Of course, this means making sure that you know how to operate any equipment you will be using, as well as organising yourself, the group and everyone else involved during production so that you make the best use of time and facilities.

You will need to be flexible; equipment can go wrong, the weather can be against you, important individuals can be ill. If you have planned properly, you will have anticipated some problems and developed ideas of how to work around them. Remember, the quality of your finished product depends directly on the quality of all the work you do in the pre-production stage. If you have prepared properly, the production stage should be straight-forward.

**Post-production** in the media industries usually refers to work that is done by specialist people such as film and video-tape editors after studio or location production work is finished. For present purposes, it is best to think of this as the stage at which you 'tidy up' your project and then present it to your intended

| TITLE |
| --- |
| BASIC STORY/IDEA/SITUATION |
| MAIN CHARACTERS/EVENTS/LOCATIONS |

| | ADVANTAGES | DISADVANTAGES |
| --- | --- | --- |
| VIDEO | | |
| FILM | | |
| RADIO | | |
| PRINT | | |
| OTHERS | | |
| OTHERS | | |

For our project (title) . . .

The most appropriate medium is . . .

Because . . .

*Figure 7.1*

audience. You will need to think about how successful the project has been in achieving what you set out to do. The place for this will be in your log-book or diary, but you might also want to tape any group discussions you have as part of this post-production evaluation.

Keeping these three stages in mind – pre-production, production and post-production – let's go on to look in more detail at what is involved in working with different media.

## Radio

Producing a radio programme is a very attractive option for any practical work, not least because most schools and colleges have some sound-recording equipment. Access to ¼-inch reel-to-reel tape recorder is ideal, but you can get very good results using just a simple audio-cassette recorder. With more than one machine, you can edit, and produce more sophisticated programmes. Again, if you can get an external microphone, you will get better results than you will relying on an internal mike.

Before you finally decide to work with sound, it is worth thinking about the advantages and disadvantages of radio as a medium. It is a good idea to make a list of what radio can do well, and of its limitations; in Figure 7.2 we have started you off!

Doing this will help you plan and produce a programme that makes the very best use of radio's advantages as a medium; it should also help you to avoid trying to do things that could be better done, for example, in print or on video.

If it can be arranged, a visit to a local radio station will be extremely useful; most local radio stations and the people who work there are very helpful, especially to young people who are interested in radio!

Let's suppose that you decide to make a radio programme on your local Citizen's Advice Bureau (CAB), looking not only at the sort of help it can offer, but also asking members of the public how it has helped them. These are the detailed stages you will need to go through:

### 1. Planning

From the beginning, you need to think about how your radio programme is going to be shaped and structured, what sort of information you want it to include, and how long the programme will be. Will it include some music? What sort, and where? How many presenters? How many interviews with CAB volunteers and with members of the public? What is the mode of address and overall 'feel' of the programme to be? Who is the audience for the programme, and what will they expect the programme to do? Whether working on your own, or as part of a group, these are questions which you must have answers to before you move on to the next stage.

### 2. Research

Once you have planned the broad outlines of your programme, you need to gather information on just what the CAB actually does, the type of help it offers people, when it is open, if the help is free, and so on. Of course, for this you will need to contact them at a very early stage, to see if they agree to help you make your programme! You will also need to, if you think you want to, arrange with some people who have been helped by the CAB about being interviewed. Needless to say, this requires a great deal of tact and skill.

As well as researching your programme information, you should give a great deal of thought to your programme style. You will have thought about this earlier in the planning stage, but it is very useful to listen to programmes of a similar genre or type on, say, Radio 4 or your local radio station. If you are working in a group, it is worth doing this as a group, and then discussing aspects of style and presentation.

| RADIO | |
|---|---|
| **Advantages** | **Limitations** |
| It feels live and immediate. | You cannot see people or places. |
| etc | etc |
| etc | etc |

*Figure 7.2*

## 3. Scripting

When you have got all the information you need, both for your programme content and style, you will need to begin writing a script. Although there are set conventions for radio scripting, it is important to realise that, what a script does is to give you a detailed 'map' of where you are going. It involves selecting what to put into your programme and, just as important, what to leave out. It is at this scripting stage that vital decisions have to be made. As we have already said, if you have more than one cassette recorder, of if you have the facilities to transfer material on to a ¼-inch reel-to-reek tape recorder, you can make a better job of editing a programme by inserting or re-recording the material on to the master tape and your script will constantly remind you of the agreed order in which you need to edit. If you only have access to one recorder the script is just as important, because you will have to get the sequence of recordings exactly right as you record each segment in its correct order. Of course, in the case of this particular programme on the CAB, you would be able to write down the presenter's words in advance. Naturally, though, you won't be able to do that for any interviews you record, because you won't know exactly what people will say. Interviews like this can be a problem; on the whole, if you want to record interviews, you will need some basic facility to edit your materials.

Let's imagine that you want to make the programme as it might actually be heard on radio, following one programme and coming before another. Above all, your script must bear in mind radio's need for variety in its sounds; you will need music, different voices, different background noises, different levels of volume and different segment lengths if your listener is not to get bored. Keeping this in mind, your script might look like the example to the right.

Of course, a script is not a tablet of stone. Even for a programme like this, it is possible and quite acceptable to make changes to your script, and the programme, as new ideas crop up, or interesting material is collected. The real value of a detailed script is that it gives you a good sense of where you are going.

If you do have access to more than one recorder and can edit material between the two machines, you might think of using cue sheets for your presenter, like the ones in Figures 7.4 and 7.5. These are used by presenters on live radio as a way of knowing when to speak before or after a pre-recorded item, or by newsreaders in-between pre-recorded items on audio cartridge. You might find them a valuable way of helping you to organise your material and so produce a more polished programme.

## 4. Recording

It should be obvious that, if you have done your research, planning and organisation properly, the actual recording of material is fairly straight-forward. Do make sure, though, that you test that the machine is working properly before you begin to record the material you want. Whenever possible, choose the best acoustic conditions to record in, so that sound you don't want (like passing traffic or other

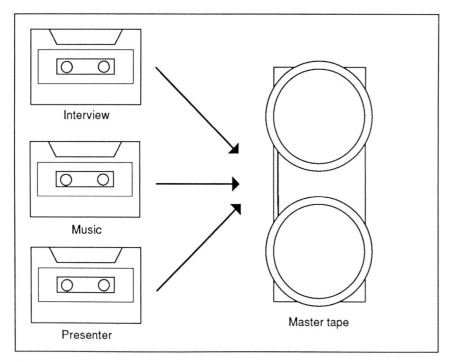

**Figure 7.3**

**RADIO WHATEVER**

*Citizen's Advice Bureau*

| 1 | MUSIC (10 secs): | *Fade down to . . .* |
|---|---|---|
| 2 | ANNOUNCER: | And now Radio Whatever presents its weekly look at you and your community. This week, the Citizen's Advice Bureau. Your presenter is Jillian Riley. |
| 3 | SERIES TITLE MUSIC (15 secs): | *Fade down to . . .* |
| 4 | PRESENTER: | Hello everyone and welcome to the programme, which this week looks at the work of the Citizen's Advice Bureau. We went along to the local office of the CAB to find out about the sort of help and advice it can offer people. |
| 5 | BACKGROUND NOISE AND ACTIVITY (5 secs): | |
| 6 | PRESENTER: | It's ten o'clock on a Tuesday morning and already the offices of the Citizen's Advice Bureau are full of people . . . And so on. |

people talking) doesn't find its way on to your tape. Try to avoid rooms that have an echo, particularly for interviews. Always do a test run, and then test your actual recording by listening to it before you leave; it can be embarrassing to have to come back again, and it may not be possible! If you have an external microphone, try it out a few times to see what position gives the best sound level and clearest recording.

## 5. Editing

If you do have use of more than one machine, this is the stage at which you put together your finished programme, simply by re-recording the different segments on to the 'master' tape,

---

SHEET — CUE SHEET

Programme ....................................................................................  Tx ....................................................  Time ...........................

SUBJECT .......................................................................................  Rpt ..................................................  Time ...........................

Duration .......................................................................................  Producer/Interviewer ..................................................................

Cue:

IN ............................................................................

OUT ............................................................................

Back Anno:

*Figure 7.4*

as described earlier. Remember to follow your script and any changes you may have made to it. Try to make sure that you get the same level and balance of sound as you transfer material on to the master tape, by testing it before you go for the final recording.

Remember to make sure that your finished programme has plenty of variety of sound. This should have been possible by using the mixture of music and different voices, background noises, different lengths for different segments, and all the elements you can hear by listening to broadcast radio programmes.

Finally, when you are sure that you have produced the best programme within the constraints you are working with, get people to listen to your tape and invite their constructive comments. When you have done this, make sure that you have properly reflected all the processes you have gone through, and all the thoughts about using radio as a medium, in your log-book or production diary.

## Video

Producing a video programme is an option that is very appealing, partly because television remains the dominant popular medium. Certainly, making a video can be a very rewarding experience, but you do need to think very carefully about exactly what is involved. It can be a long and complex process, sometimes a frustrating one, and it will take up a lot of your time! It is definitely a group activity, though it does offer plenty of scope for doing a range of tasks both individually and as part of the group.

Although some schools and colleges are beginning to get access to expensive editing equipment, most are lucky to have a single camera. It you can use more than one video recorder, then you will be able to crash-edit your material, by re-recording material from the first machine on to the second machine in a similar way to using two audio-cassette recorders. Inevitably, this produces results that are less than 'professional', but you will experience the process of editing. If you don't have access to more than one machine, you will need to edit in camera, which means

---

SHEET — CUE SHEET

Programme .....You and Your Community......................... Tx ............................................... Time ...............................
SUBJECT .....Citizen's Advice Bureau......................... Rpt ............................................. Time ...............................
Duration ...................................................................................... Producer/Interviewer .....Jillian Riley...........................

Cue:

        Hallo everyone and welcome to the programme, which this

        week looks at the Citizen's Advice Bureau. We went along

        to the local office of the CAB to find out about the sort

        of help and advice it can offer people.

                                          IN .....Background noise and activity. (5 secs)

                                          OUT ..as above..............................................................

Back Anno:  It's ten o'clock on a Tuesday morning and already the offices of

               the Citizen's Advice Bureau are full of people . . .

*Figure 7.5*

shooting your material in the order or sequence you intend to show it on television.

As with radio, before you finally decide whether to opt for video, it is important to think about the things that video does well, and the things it is not so good at. Your comments will obviously apply to television as well. It is a good idea to get your ideas down on paper, and discuss them as a group. (See Figure 7.6.)

| VIDEO | |
|---|---|
| **Advantages** | **Disadvantages** |
| | |

*Figure 7.6*

Modern video equipment, especially the new generation of camcorders, is capable of producing excellent quality pictures and sound. Remember though, that whilst you will want your programme to look and sound as polished as possible, it will not look like professionally broadcast programmes; the important element lies in experiencing the processes you will go through in making your programme.

As an example, let's imagine that you want to produce a video about the sorts of food that people in your school or college eat, whether they eat in the canteen or bring their own food. You particularly want to draw attention to the importance of healthy diet.

In broad terms, here are some of the stages you will need to go through in making your video:

### 1. Planning

As with radio, you will need to think about the overall shape and structure of your programme. This will be determined by who you think your audience will be, and by your ideas about what video as a medium can do well, remembering that it is a combination of sound and pictures (including graphics). Suppose the point of your video is to encourage young people to think about the need for a nutritious diet. You might decide that your audience will want a programme that has pace, that they will want any information to be presented in a light-hearted way, and that they will expect some music. All of this centres around an appropriate mode of address which is suitable for your programme content, and which will keep your audience involved in the programme. In any case, avoid being too ambitious about the length of your programme. A well made video lasting 5 minutes or less is much preferable to 20 minutes of disjointed and rambling chaos.

### 2. Research

As with radio, this involves gathering information which will be useful both for programme content and programme style. You will probably want to conduct some interviews. Think about who to interview and where to interview them. How will you present 'solid facts'? You might want to use graphics, so that you can display written information on the screen when you need to. Think about the visual style of your video, the audience it is aimed at, and look at examples of programmes on broadcast television which are aimed at a youth audience. Look into what you understand by a so-called documentary style, if that seems appropriate. What would the difference be if you wanted a more fictional style of presentation? Music will probably be important, so you will need to think about appropriate types of music. People and locations need researching and organising!

### 3. Storyboard

When you feel that you have a fairly clear idea of the shape, content and style of your video, you will find it useful to put your ideas on to a storyboard. There are different types of storyboard, but you will find a useful example in Figure 7.7. The basic idea is to give you, in visual form, a clear sense of how your programme is going to look and be organised. Like a radio script, it is a sort of map for you to follow when it comes to shooting your footage. Because video is a visual medium, a storyboard is a better way of doing this than a written script. It should include a visual of each intended shot, which will indicate the framing and composition, camera angle and how near or far the camera is to be placed in relation to the people or objects being shot. The storyboard should show, for example, whether a long-shot (LS), mid-shot (MS), or a close-shot (CS) is needed. It should also tell you the duration of each shot, or how long it lasts. Any speech, dialogue, music or other sound effects should be indicated, though you should bear in mind that you can usually dub-over sound at a later stage, using the audio-dub facility that is on most video recorders. The storyboard will also indicate any graphic material you want to use, such as a title or the names of the production group. These will need to be prepared before shooting, of course.

It is a good idea to do a draft or rough-copy storyboard, talk

Figure 7.7

PROGRAMME TITLE _____

GROUP NAMES _____

| Shot No. | Picture | Type of shot and duration | Sound |
|---|---|---|---|
| 1 | | Caption 10 Secs | MUSIC - 'Food Glorious Food'<br><br>Fade to . . . |
| 2 | | LS 12 Secs | VOICE-OVER - 'A hot summer's day, a visit to an ice-cream parlour. What could be more natural?' |
| 3 | | MS 8 Secs | MUSIC - 'Food Glorious Food'<br><br>Fade down to . . . |
| 4 | | CS 6 secs | VOICE-OVER - 'And what could be more glorious than Knickerbocker Glory?' |

through your ideas as a group, make any changes you think are needed, and then go on to produce a neat final version which can be used during shooting. It would be useful to put copies of rough drafts and the final storyboard in your log-book, together with comments on why the changes were made.

When you have written and drawn out your finished storyboard, you should use it as a guide for making all the organisational arrangements which will be necessary. For example, you will perhaps want to shoot in the school or college canteen; the storyboard will be invaluable in letting you plan just when this should happen. This leads us on to the next stage.

## 4. Shooting

Before you can begin shooting your footage, you need to do two things:

1. Get to know how the camera operates so that you can use it effectively.
2. Work out a shooting schedule.

Before you begin to shoot your video, it is essential that you know how to use the camera properly. This means practising with it by doing very small-scale exercises, so that you become familiar with the camera you will be using. Each camera is slightly different, so it really does pay to practise with it before you begin to shoot your project.

When you are happy with using the camera, you need to organise a shooting schedule. This means arranging locations and people in the order you want to shoot them, when you want to shoot them. Obviously, this must be done before you can begin shooting, and it is a good idea to get the arrangements down on paper.

Figure 7.8 shows a simple form that will serve as a reminder of your shooting schedule.

When everything is organised and you have written out your shooting schedule, you are ready to go ahead with the actual shooting. Remember, though, that the success of your programme depends directly on how good a job you have made of all the pre-shooting planning and organisation.

Using the camera, especially if you have already practised with it, is fairly straight-forward, but remember to make the most of the best lighting and acoustic conditions available. As with using an audio-cassette recorder, always check that the material you want has actually been recorded!

## 5. Editing

If you are editing in camera, you will need to shoot each scene in the order in which it will appear on the screen. This has obvious limitations, but good results can be got with careful planning and organisation if you avoid being too ambitious in your project.

With more than one video recorder, you can connect them together and crash-edit your material, so that it can be put together in a different order from that in which it was shot following your storyboard. This ability to crash-edit does give much greater flexibility in your shooting schedule, because you are free from having to shoot everything in sequence. Whether you are editing-in-camera or crash editing, this is the stage at which you can audio-dub any music or speech on to your tape, by using the audio-dub facility that most video recorders have. This offers a lot of creative possibilities, and you don't have to always use the raw sound recorded during shooting. Again, your storyboard will detail if and when you want to audio-dub sound over the original sound.

Finally, you need to evaluate your programme by discussing it and seeing how far it has achieved what you hoped it would. Have the confidence to show it to an audience and invite constructive comments. You may not have produced a programme like you see on broadcast television, you may wish that you had more time to improve it, but almost certainly you will have produced something that you can be rightly proud of!

| Programme title _____ | | | |
|---|---|---|---|
| Group names _____ | | | |
| **Date** | **Time** | **Location** | **Shooting/Storyboard No.** |
|  |  |  |  |

*Figure 7.8*

## Print

Print refers to practical projects that may be booklets, posters, magazines, comics or newspapers. It can include both written and visual material. The advantage of print as a project is that it doesn't rely on such specialist equipment as video and radio do, although the production processes which you need to go through are very similar. Access to a computer and a desk-top publishing programme, linked to a printer, will give very polished results, but you can get very good results using typewritten and even handwritten material. What you will learn about print media will be just as valuable whether your finished product is handwritten or professionally printed!

When radio and then television came along, some people forecast that the print media would wither away, but today the circulation figures for newspapers, magazines and specialist journals are as high as ever. What advantages do the print media continue to have that are not shared by video and radio? What are the limitations of the print media? Before you decide to work in this medium, it is important to think about these questions. Writing down your thoughts will be helpful (Figure 7.9).

| PRINT | |
|-------|-------------|
| **Advantages** | **Disadvantages** |
| | |
| | |
| | |
| | |

**Figure 7.9**

Let's imagine that working individually or as part of a group, you want to produce a promotional leaflet about GCSE media studies, aimed at youngsters who might be thinking of doing the subject as one of their options. These are the stages you will need to go through.

### 1. Planning and research

You will need to gather information about media studies as a subject, about what it will involve in terms of time and activities. As well as thinking about the content of your leaflet, you will need to think about an appropriate style and format. You could approach this by collecting and discussing as many different examples of printed publicity material as you can. You should remember that you will probably want to use both written and visual material, so gather as many different examples of both as you can. You must think very carefully about your intended audience or readership, and about the leaflet's language, mode of address and style of presentation. Discuss ideas for the overall design of the leaflet. What size will it be? Will it be folded in some way? Will copy appear on both sides of the paper? Will you include visual material, and where? At this stage, it is a good idea to produce several rough 'mock-ups' to use as a basis for discussion about what is the best overall design and style.

### 2. Writing

When you have some firm ideas about the basic style and design, you need to start writing some draft copy. Remember that you need to balance information and mode of address; what you are saying with how you say it. This is determined by what you have decided about your target readership, about appropriate use of language, and about the appropriate style. At this early stage, it does not matter if individual written pieces are too long, because they can be edited or re-written later.

### 3. Visual material

You will have made a decision earlier about any visual material you want to include. You will need to think more carefully about what type of visual material to use, why you want to use it, what purpose it is going to serve. You may want to use or take some photographs, but you could also use sketches, cartoons, or other illustrative material such as a collage. When the editorial decisions have been made, the visual material needs to be produced.

### 4. Preparation of copy

When you have produced your first-draft written copy and your visual material, you need to think about presentation and lay-out, about how you will arrange the material on each page in a way that will attract and hold a reader. Even if you are producing hand-written copy in your finished leaflet, you have to decide on factors such as the size and type of writing (or of the typewriting and print if you have access to these), the length of each line, how much space to leave between lines and between different sub-sections, as well as the relationship between written copy and visual material.

When all these decisions have been taken, and you have seen how each piece of rough copy fits into your agreed design and lay-out, you should go on to produce final-version copy, re-writing or cutting down where this is necessary. Each piece of finished copy should be numbered, ready for paste-up.

## 5. Paste-up and copying

Having rewritten or preferably retyped your final version copy so that it fits in exactly with your agreed design and lay-out, you need to physically prepare each page so that it takes each piece of separate copy. This is done by drawing guidelines on the paper, using a blue non-reproducing pencil, to show where each piece of separate written and visual copy goes on the page. Each piece of separate copy should be prepared to exactly the size indicated on the page guidelines. Figure 7.10 shows an example of a page ready for paste-up:

Once the copy has been pasted down in the correct places, the pasted-up leaflet is ready for what is known professionally as 'camera-ready copy', the stage before printing. For our purposes, you could present the pasted-up pages as they are, but if you can manage to get access to a photocopier, you can run off as many 'printed' copies as you want. Photocopying produces very good results that will do justice to the hard work you've put into your project!

Finally, you need to discuss your finished product, test it out on your target readership, and come to some conclusions about how well you have done. Most important of all, you will want to discuss what you have learnt by doing your print media project!

## Other media

Although we have looked in detail at the processes involved in producing practical work in radio, video and print, it is just as possible to work in one of a range of other media. For example, you may have access to, and want to use, 8mm film. Although you would have to recognise some of the differences between using a film camera and a video camera, you would still use a very similar approach to the one detailed for video production. You might want to produce a photoplay which combines photographs and other visual material with a written text, or a tape-slide programme, combining slides with a synchronised audio-tape.

The important thing to remember is, that whichever medium you work in, the quality and success of the finished product depends directly on all the preparatory work you do. The stages and processes outlined in detail for radio, video and print will be similar if you decide to work with another medium.

Above all, you should try and relate your experience in practical production work to the ideas you have come across during the whole of your media studies course. A permanent record of your experiences, such as a log-book or a diary, will help you not just to record what, how and when you did something, but will also help you to evaluate and reflect upon working with your particular medium.

As well as doing something which is very satisfying and very enjoyable, practical production work should have increased your understanding of the media products you come across every day of your life:

I hear and I forget,
I see and I remember,
I *do* and I *understand*.

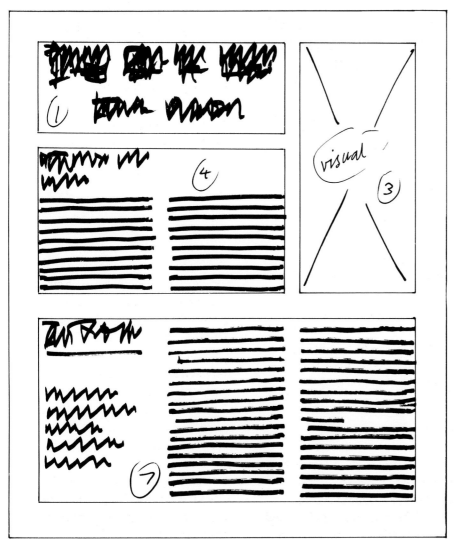

*Figure 7.10*

# INDEX

# ACKNOWLEDGEMENTS

The author would like to thank Irene Ansell for typing the manuscript.

We are grateful to the following for permission to reproduce photographs and copyright material:
*Airways,* Spring 1987, quarterly journal of the IBA, page 62; BBC Enterprises, page 76 *below:* BBC Picture Publicity, page 103 *above left; Campaign,* page 32 *above;* Campaign for Press & Broadcasting Freedom, Media Manifesto, page 129; J. Allan Cash Photolibrary, page 79 *below right;* Channel 4, page 80; (c)1988 M.C. Escher Heirs/Cordon Art-Baarn-Holland, page 10 *above;* Daily Express, page 78 *below*; Daily Mirror, pages 84 *above*, 86; Daily Star, page 32 *below*; Fresh Air, page 42 *below;* Granada Television Limited, pages 64 *below right,* 95; Sally & Richard Greenhill, page 84 *below right;* Guardian, page 25, 32; extract from J. Hind & S. Mosco: *Rebel Radio,* Pluto 1985, page 40; extract from *IBA Television & Radio Yearbook 1988* pages 45, 46; *The Independent*, pages 15, 16, 61; Independent Television Publications Limited, page 26; JICNARS National Readership Survey, page 110; Katz Eyes, page 77 *above* (Snap photo, Los Angeles); Keystone Collection, page 64 *below left*; Kobal Collection, pages 19, 90 *below*, 91 *below*, 103 *centre; The Observer,* page 29; Manchester Free Press, page 42 *above; Media Week,* page 30 *below; Mirror TV Week*, page 30 *above*, Paramount Pictures Corp, page 91 *above*, New Realm Entertainments Ltd, page 114; *Radio Times*, pages 11 *below*, 55, 73, 96–7; Scottish TV plc, page 20; *The Sun,* pages 17, 78 *above; Sunday Sport,* page 61; *Sunday Times,* page 59 *below; TV Times,* pages 26, 102, 103 *right; Today,* page 61; 20th Century Fox, page 90 *above;* Universal Oak Picture, page 23 *above;* U.I.P. page 92 *below;* Wrangler, page 117; Leon Griffiths: *Arthur Daley's Guide to Doing it Right,* Willow Books Collins, page 64 *centre right;* Illustration by Mike and John Gilkes reproduced from *Inside Information* by Jacquetta Megarry with the permission of BBC Enterprises Ltd.

We are grateful to the following for permission to reproduce copyright material:
British Broadcasting Corporation for an extract from *BBC Audience Research Findings 1986: Eastenders: The Research Contribution*; The British Code of Advertising Practice for an extract from Appendix 1 *Advertising Standards Authority Code* (October 1985); Comedia Publishing for an extract from *News Limited* by B Whitaker (1981); Constable & Co Ltd for an extract from *The Media in Britain* by Jeremy Tunstall; Guardian Newspapers Ltd for an extract from the article 'Star gone to the sewers' in *The Guardian* 11.8.87; Listener Publications Ltd for an extract from *The Listener* 22.5.86 and an extract from the article 'Selling His Soul' by Andrew Goodwin in *The Listener* 1.10.87; Macdonald & Co (Publishers) Ltd for extracts from *Adventures in the Screen Trade* by William Goldman; Methuen & Co for an extract from *Introduction to Communication Studies* by J Fiske (1982); The Observer Ltd for an extract from *The Observer* 24.1.82; Thames Television PLC for an extract from *Thames TV Annual Report 1986* (c) Thames Television PLC 1986; Times Newspapers Ltd for an extract from the article 'Future Shock' by Rod Allen in *The Sunday Times* 7.12.80 (c) Times Newspapers Ltd 1988.